A Sensitive Liberal's
Guide to Life

How to Banter With Your Barista,

Hug Mindfully, and Relate to Friends

Who Choose Kids Over Dogs

GOTHAM
BOOKS

A Sensitive Liberal's Guide to Life

By

THE UPTIGHT SEATTLEITE

GOTHAM BOOKS
Published by Penguin Group (USA) Inc.
375 Hudson Street, New York, New York 10014, U.S.A.
Penguin Group (Canada), 90 Eglinton Avenue East, Suite 700, Toronto, Ontario M4P 2Y3, Canada
(a division of Pearson Penguin Canada Inc.); Penguin Books Ltd, 80 Strand, London WC2R 0RL,
England; Penguin Ireland, 25 St Stephen's Green, Dublin 2, Ireland (a division of Penguin Books Ltd);
Penguin Group (Australia), 250 Camberwell Road, Camberwell, Victoria 3124, Australia (a division of
Pearson Australia Group Pty Ltd); Penguin Books India Pvt Ltd, 11 Community Centre, Panchsheel
Park, New Delhi – 110 017, India; Penguin Group (NZ), 67 Apollo Drive, Rosedale, North Shore 0632,
New Zealand (a division of Pearson New Zealand Ltd); Penguin Books (South Africa) (Pty) Ltd, 24
Sturdee Avenue, Rosebank, Johannesburg 2196, South Africa

Penguin Books Ltd, Registered Offices: 80 Strand, London WC2R 0RL, England

Published by Gotham Books, a member of Penguin Group (USA) Inc.

First printing, March 2010
3 5 7 9 10 8 6 4 2

Gotham Books and the skyscraper logo are trademarks of Penguin Group (USA) Inc.

LIBRARY OF CONGRESS CATALOGING-IN-PUBLICATION DATA
Stoesz, David.
A sensitive liberal's guide to life : how to banter with your barista, hug mindfully, and relate to friends
who choose kids over dogs / by An Uptight Seattleite [David Stoesz].
p. cm.
ISBN 978-1-592-40529-9 (pbk.)
1. Conduct of Life—Humor.   2. Liberals—Humor.   3. American wit and humor.   I. Title.
PN6231.C6142S76   2010
814'.6—dc22   2009032524

Printed in the United States of America
Set in Guardi LT STD with Goudy Sans
Designed by Sabrina Bowers

To Kako, Boodle, and Fefer

Contents

Let Me Introduce Myself Real Quick

Why seek advice from a Seattleite? You may have read stories in *The New York Times* travel section about Seattle's seafood, progressive politics, and funky neighborhoods. And I'm out to prove that, though we may know a bit more about recycling than you, we definitely still know how to get fun-*kay*! So I hope we can go through the friendly reminders collected here in a spirit of open-minded exploration.

I'm not making out that Seattle is some kind of perfect place though. Seattle is no Portland. Did you know that Portland has a train system powered entirely by magnets and gravity? That its downtown is a no-car, leash-free meadow; that in place of the supermarkets driven out by their No Chain Store Act they have a network of cooperatively run farmer's markets; and that pedaling silhouettes crisscross the sky in glass-enclosed bikeways? "Hamster tunnels," the locals affectionately call them. They're all paid for with a carbon tax levied against the city's suburbs.

You might object that none of these things are true. Well, facts can be PRET-ty slippery things. So-called "objective reality" has been extensively problematized. Besides, I think we need to get beyond the whole "who's right and who's wrong" mentality here. Don't worry though, that's one of the things we're going to work on in this book.

But gosh, where are my manners? I haven't even introduced myself properly and I'm already starting to ramble. So let me back up and say, first of all, welcome to the book! Now that this book is in your hands, you may wonder what it's all about. Well, as an advice columnist for the *Seattle Weekly*, I act as the city's life coach, counseling its citizens on everything from silly little dilemmas in the coffee shop to this whole crazy business of being human. From "what's the darn meaning of it all?" to "how much do I tip?" The column is a place where readers convene every week to exchange my ideas and then go on their way, refreshed and replenished. So some of what I'll be sharing here will be letters directly from the column. Other times it'll be just be you and me, hanging out and rappin'. Like we're doing right now.

Will reading this book make you a more sensitive, globally aware person and lead you toward an enriched spiritual life? A life attuned to an infinity of harmonious cycles, from the beating of your heart to the spinning of the stars? Only if I do my part and not press too hard here. A light touch is key. A light touch still has friction though, and you just might experience sparks of static electricity between your eyes and the page. But the most important thing here is fun, and we're definitely going to have that. Heck, sometimes our discussions about race, the environment, and body shame are going to get nuttier than a box of crackers!

One quick thing to address before we "get down" to it (I *told* you we'd have funk, er, fun!). Where do I get my ideas? Lots of people wonder that. Even if they don't ask. Well, for one thing, I carry a little notebook around. A Moleskine, the legendary notebook that's held the ideas of such artists and freethinkers as Picasso, Hemingway, and Bruce Chatwin. I don't think it's necessary for everyone to carry a Moleskine. But me, I guess you could say I'm kind of an ideas geek.

You may sometimes see me in the morning with my Moleskine, porcelain Swan Neck pen pressed pensively to my lips, gazing out the window of the No. 5 bus as it rumbles over the Aurora Bridge high above Lake Union. Maybe you'll notice the dreamy look in my eyes as I grasp in my silly way at the wisdom in the air above Mount Rainier. If a wry little smile suddenly flashes across my face, it may mean I've wrestled a helpful little nugget out of the ether. Like the page I've turned to in my Moleskine where the words *Let go!* are underlined three times. Is this a reminder for myself or my readers? Both, of course. I find it's helpful to let my private and public jottings flow into one another. The way ALL THINGS CONSIDERED uses a tender, tinkly little variation on its theme music to transition from a story about poverty to a personal essay segment. The music indicates how we should feel about poverty (sad) and also gives us a meditative space to *Let go!* and relax into the folksy ramblings of someone remembering the smell of her grandmother's kitchen. That's why I've made some of my private jottings from my Moleskine available throughout the book. If you don't at first see how my private musings are "relevant," that's OK! You will! Because I sense you want to grow. That you *can* grow.

Uh-oh! We haven't even gotten started and I'm already breaking our little Covenant of Fun by getting all heavy on you. From now on I'll always try to cushion my words with that all-important fun factor, because I know it's tough to find out you're wrong. At least I imagine it is.

Diversity

Skiing black men, sneezing Indians

Sometimes when I'm using chopsticks to eat bi bim bop at my local Korean restaurant, I notice other people using spoons to eat their own bi bim bop. I smile at them and their spoons. My smile says, "Hey, great for you! You're branching out and trying something new, even if that's a little uncomfortable for you. You might find that your experience of another culture is even more enriching if you try using chopsticks. Just a thought! Enjoy your meal!" That really sums up what we're going to discuss here: how the buffet of diversity is best enjoyed with unfamiliar utensils.

Before we get into a discussion of how to relate to people of all sorts—be they differently hued or simply given to sneezing more than seems wholesome—I want to make one thing clear: I include myself here. I don't hold myself up as someone who doesn't need this kind of advice. But since we're on the topic, I'll just throw it out there that I'm pretty much color-blind. I can't help it—I just see people, period. This one time, when I met a new co-worker? Someone asked me later what he looked like, and I didn't remember. When pressed, I could dimly recall that he was a six-foot-five Filipino squinting into the sunset, with a blood-red kerchief tied neatly about his throat. Whatever, though, right? Because what difference did it make?

Bon appétit!

Other folks, other colors

The bottom line is that all people must be respected as individuals. To that end, let's divide them into categories and talk about them in terms of these categories.

Like black men who ski. Is there something surprising about that? Co-workers who speak Spanish. Or *do* they? Sneezing Indians. What does "Indian" mean in this case?

Exactly! Your questions show how fast you're catching on, and that you're ready to meet the people in our first group. OK, roll 'em Murray! (There isn't really a guy in a booth named Murray who makes the letters appear on the page, but isn't it fun to pretend there is?)

I dread the skiing and snowboarding season. For months on end, my co-workers will arrive on Monday mornings aglow with smug joy at how great the "powder" was up at Crystal. Oh, and it's all totally sunny up there, too, they'll tell us losers who spent the weekend down here below the clouds. I don't exult over the novel I read or the great movie I saw while they were "shredding" or whatever, so why do I have to listen to them?

SANS SKIS SAM

Dear Sam,

Speaking as a black man, I resent your assumption that I don't ski, and that I will therefore share your anti-skiing position. Aren't I as likely to ski as anyone else? I can hear you objecting that I am not, in fact, a black man. I didn't say I was. What I said was that, *speaking* as a black man, I resented your assumption. There's a difference. See, Sam, words have power. The power to hurt, yes, and that sadly seems to be your focus. But also the power to heal. To bring us together. And to that, speaking as a human being with a rainbow soul, I say, "Right on."

A co-worker has serious allergies. When he gets a particularly bad sneezing fit, he might sneeze, no lie, thirty times in a row. He sometimes gets up and stands outside to finish his sneezing marathon. It seems like he wants privacy on these occasions, but I also feel like I should offer some kind of support. Also, and I don't know if this is relevant, he's Indian.

WHA-CHOO I DO?

Dear Wha-choo,

Don't just let the poor guy suffer in peace! Follow him outside. Say "bless you" after every sneeze. But take care not to become too mechanical in your blessings. You have to show you really mean it. Make eye contact (as best you can with someone whose head is jerking spastically). Keep up a line of sympathetic patter that shows you're fully present for him: "Bless you! Bless you! Bless you! Oh my goodness, that was a big one, bless you again! . . . Whoa, Nelly, that's quite a streak you've got going! Bless you one more time!" (You should avoid the word "God," for obvious reasons.)

If by "Indian" you meant your co-worker is a Native American (remember, we all have to be more careful about how we use our words!), you could express your support with a lighthearted reference that he will be sure to appreciate: "I think even Geronimo heard that one, brother!" If you meant he's an Indian from India, you could say: "I think you're getting all your sneezing out of the way for this incarnation and the next one, too!" When his sneezing fit has passed, offer some calming words to plant positive images of wholeness and harmony in his mind and help him regain his equilibrium. Pat him on the shoulder and say, "Seashells and lilacs, my friend. Seashells, lilacs, and gentle midnight rain."

I recently needed some Spanish text translated. So I approached a co-worker—a guy with a Hispanic name whom I'd heard trading various Spanish squibs with another co-worker who is also Hispanic. Well, it turned out those squibs were all he knew. My Spanish was probably better than his. But the thing is, everyone in the surrounding cubes who heard this exchange reacted like I'd committed some egregious offense. But why is it racist to think that a Hispanic guy might know Spanish?

FAUX PAUL

Dear Paul,

Your reasoning seems compelling. Your co-worker was speaking in Spanish, so you assumed he speaks Spanish. But the key word here is "assume." You made an assumption involving someone's ethnicity, and everyone in your office knew it. Your defensive tone shows that you know it, too.

Maybe it's too late for this time, but you can start planning for the next situation that's identical to this one in every way. Here's what you should do: Pick up a little more Spanish yourself. (You may even find it's exhilarating to free your mind from the constraints of English. Those of us who have studied other languages do tend to conclude with amused chagrin that our native language is a poor instrument indeed.) Then approach your co-worker with a friendly Spanish phrase or two.

But keep fresh in your mind the fires of mortification that seized your flesh once before. Approach cautiously. Enter his squib flow slowly, tenderly. Say something anyone would know, such as *"Hola, amigo!"* Next, gradually introduce more complex sentences, such as *"Que hora es, amigo?"* Then start really mixing it up. Intentionally misuse the subjunctive case while peering searchingly into his face to see if he catches it. And when you're sure he actually does have some competence in Spanish, open the tequila, pull the curtain on the mariachi band you've hired for the occasion, and dance around the room wearing a sombrero. Isn't that sort of where you wanted to go with this? That's the question I'd like to leave you with.

Chinese people and their towns

I've noticed that people in other cities persist in using the term "Chinatown." Here in Seattle we say "The International District." People refer to this neighborhood when discussing where the best place to get dim sum is. They usually mention some place packed with tourists. I smile to encourage their continued pursuit of food prepared by foreigners, and silently hope they'll discover a more authentic experience. Such as can be found at the small, out-of-the-way place I go for the *real* best dim sum in town.

Anyway, "Chinatown." I know it seems like an innocuous term, a richly historical term, even. But if the neighborhood is "Chinatown," why not call its residents "Chinamen"? That term has history, too. Maybe you want them to wear those little pajamas and do laundry? And perhaps lay a bit of railroad track? But of course you wouldn't say "a Chinaman" any more than you'd say "a colored," "a gay," or "a Jew." I'm actually not quite clear on the Jew thing. But it does sound harsh somehow, doesn't it? "He's a Jew, she's a Jew, they're all Jews." But you know what? I'm pretty sure we shouldn't even be talking about this, so never mind. Also, I apologize, if that's called for.

I recently had my appendix out, by the way, and my surgeon was an Asian. And female. Not that that matters at all. I actually didn't even notice. But an Asian woman wielding the scalpel of Western medicine on a Caucasian male does raise some fascinating issues. I'm talking male/female, dominant/submissive, penetrated/ penetrator, knife/phallus. On my last visit with Dr. Yuen, I tried to explore this with her a little bit. Purely as a matter of professional interest. Maybe I overestimated her intellectual curiosity. At any rate, I thought calling security was a bit of an overreaction on her part.

✳

I'm glad that some of my readers are a bit more bold when it comes to facing Asian questions though. Like this fellow who raises an uncomfortable one indeed:

Sensitivity exercise #42

Hey, did you know that the proper term for that fruit is *nashi*? "Asian pear" implies that Asia is a single cultural monolith. We all need to be a little more careful about how we label things. To that end, let's give these exercises a try:

1. Take a break from labeling altogether.
The next time you bite into a *nashi*, instead of mentioning the oppressively schematic name of this fruit, say, "This is delicious!" or simply, "This!"

2. Spend the day in a post-verbal realm.
Let the power of a universal human smile do your talking. If you must vocalize, improvise with a series of grunts and clicks. Not to disparage those languages that actually *are* a series of grunts and clicks. Or to exempt them, either. I'm language-neutral when it comes to calling out violators. As one of my recent sandwich boards put it: "End Unmindful Grunting!"

Do you have any idea why ads that feature a mixed-race couple usually show a white male and an Asian female? This is especially evident in real-estate ads. Why isn't it an Asian male with a white female? Are they not welcome in those posh downtown condos or new suburban developments? What kind of lame Pacific Rim city is this?

ASIAN OUT

Dear Asian,

First of all, congratulations on your Asian heritage. I'm a big fan of your nonjudgmental spiritual traditions and commitment to education. Asians are sort of a kinder, gentler minority, aren't they? Delicious food without all the anger. That's not how I see it, of course. It's well established that I'm pretty much color-blind. But I think some people see it that way. Could that explain the lack of Asian men in real-estate ads, either accompanied by Caucasian women or not? You have to admit, it would sort of be a stereotype, wouldn't it? Like, "Oh, look at me, I'm an Asian guy, of course I can afford this fancy condo! Because I'm so good at math!" That obviously wouldn't do. A photo of a white guy/Asian woman couple, on the other hand, expresses a cosmopolitan, post-racial glamour. A tech-company white guy from Wisconsin and a second-generation Chinese-American woman smiling at the center of a snazzy downtown lifestyle, their arms around each other with warm sexual ease—is that not the very picture of tasteful aspiration? Again, I'm a bit beyond all that. I'm just talking about how other people might see it.

Should a Native American be allowed to kill a whale with a shotgun?

Honestly? I'm glad you asked. Native American history is something of a forte of mine. Indeed, you could bury my heart under the books I've read that deconstruct the manifest destiny of our tragically misguided cowboy-ism. This one time, at a Sherman Alexie book reading here in Seattle? I asked Sherm a question that I prefaced with my own personal spin on Native American history, as best I can glimpse it with a mind stumbling humbly toward a truly postcolonial perspective, a perspective that takes in with an easy grace the full landscape of ca-RAY-zy Native wisdom. The long, silent look he gave me was, I dare to believe, a tactful (so as not to exclude the rest of the audience) acknowledgment of my hard-earned Native cred.

I wouldn't even bother to tell you all of this except that I'd like to admit to a few sneaking concerns about Indians and whales. And that was just a quick little flash of my blindingly shiny "don't-mess-with-me-on-that-whole-racism-thing" badge so I can express these concerns freely.

Since Native Americans claim a right—whale hunting—that makes sensitive people squeamish, I don't think it's too much to ask them to claim it in a picturesque manner. For example, it seems to me that a hollowed-out canoe should be involved anytime a Native American kills a whale. Based on designs that go back through the generations and all that. Drums booming slowly in the background would also help, as would a chanting medicine person of some type to get the whole myth-invoking, pipe-toking deal on the road.

But when the Makah tribe won the (very valid!) right to hunt whales here in the Northwest, they used a shotgun in their whale hunts. There was a picture in the paper of a guy in the back of the canoe holding it across his legs. I have to ask, what next? If it's efficiency over tradition they want, why not a huge conveyor belt that carts whale carcasses from the ocean to factories on the shore? Profitability doesn't sound very authentic to me.

Again, I know there is danger in a Caucasian male seeming

to pass judgment on a minority group, especially one with such an impressive history of oppression, and so I say all this merely as someone whom circumstances may have blessed with an odd insight or two.

And how about that guy over there in the Palestinian scarf?

Palestinian scarf? Oh, you must mean a *keffiyeh*! Whoa, sorry, didn't mean to knock you back with my powerful consonants. If you'd like to give the correct pronunciation a try yourself, don't forget to make the throat-clearing sound that signals your awareness of the word's ethnic origins.

Hang on a minute though. Is that guy actually wearing a *keffiyeh* at all? There are *keffiyeh*-like scarfs out there. If you have any doubt, you can always seize this opportunity to practice the explosiveness of your Ks and ask, "Hey is that a *kkkkcccckkkeffiyeh*?" Have no fear of overdoing it, though it's not necessary to break into a coughing fit.

If it turns out that it is indeed a *keffiyeh*, don't feel silly because you had to ask. Instead, gently intimate that the wearer is not drap-ing the fabric in the most authentic fashion. If the little tassel things weren't flapping about in such an untidy fashion, you totally would have recognized that the *keffiyeh* was, indeed, a *keffiyeh*. Because of your familiarity and comfort with foreign accessories.

But what if the guy is an actual Middle Easterner of some sort? It's just terrible what happens over there. So much misunderstand-ing and hatred. If you don't mind, I'd rather not get too far into the specifics. It's pretty complex, after all. What's that? Why does every American politician feel compelled to reaffirm unconditional support for Israel, you ask? And how is it even possible to negoti-ate with a group like Hamas? Um, excuse me, but those sound like pretty loaded questions. Is there something offensive lurking behind those questions? Because if so, I am fully prepared to be offended. In conclusion, I would also like to reaffirm my support for greater understanding between opposing groups.

That, I hope, settles it. There is one last problem though. Let's

not say "problem." Let's say "challenge." What if you don't *know* if
the guy is an actual Middle Easterner or not? In that case, follow the
same rule you would with a woman who may or may not be pregnant: Don't say a word. Give yourself a wide berth on this. Stick to
talking about the weather even if you think the person might actually be a houndstooth-wearing Guamanian.

Other others

The point of this chapter is not to provide an encyclopedia of
categories of people and how to be sensitive to them. But in the
following letters I do want to cover at least a few of the less obvious
categories of people you may destructively think of as "The Other."
They include the handicapped and the gay. Don't be afraid of these
words. We're just talking here. Starting some conversations. Bridging
some bridges. Let's start with some five-fingered Otherness that's
closer than you might think:

> *It's a cold rainy day and I'm walking down the street holding my cof-*
> *fee cup in my right hand, and it's starting to get pretty cold. Would*
> *it be fair to ask my left to take a turn?*
>
> RIGHTY

Dear Righty,

   Let me guess: You have some discomfort around the very
idea of a dominant hand. "Dominant hand"—it has sort of
a transgressive ring, doesn't it? As if your hand dominated
YOU in some way. Hmmm . . . Actually, let's go ahead and
leave that thought alone. Look at it this way instead: On
the one hand, the expression "on the one hand," clearly
refers to your right. On the other hand, "the other hand"
could also be your right, if you were left-handed. We should
remember not to forget left-handed people, for whom the

side-neutral expression "dominant hand" was coined to begin with. Or was it? Don't we right-handers, the dominant dominant hand people, also benefit from inclusiveness?

If you said yes, you're right-o, Righty. Celebrate by being even more inclusive. Don't just ask your left hand to take a turn holding the coffee, use it to drink with, too. This is a great opportunity to develop a more informal, teasing relationship with this hand that you may at times have caused to feel invalidated. So when your left spills coffee down your chin, affectionately chide it. "Oh you!" you can say. "What am I going to do with you?" Wipe off the spill with your right, though, so your left doesn't feel bad. This is one of the rare occasions when it's better that one hand NOT know what the other is doing. By the way, you can probably avoid the spill altogether if you lock onto the cup with your lips and teeth before you sip. When it comes to drinking, your mouth is an old hand.

When I leave this hellhole called Atlanta and move to Seattle, we'll have to get together and smoke a joint and go to a coffeehouse and discuss transportation issues. I'm a civil engineer, but I'm probably going to switch careers. Unfortunately, I now have a role in urban sprawl, but I'm going to take my experience and knowledge with me when I come to Seattle to make sure we don't turn it into another Atlanta.

SEATTLE-BOUND

P.S. I'm selling my car, so hopefully I will be welcomed. I'm also homosexual.

Dear Seattle-Bound,

When you say "also homosexual," do you mean "In addition to being interested in transportation issues, I like men," or "Like you, I'm gay"? Because, if the latter, I hope you don't mind me saying that I'm not actually . . . Look, I'm straight. Straight but not narrow!

I'm not blaming you for whatever you were thinking. When people meet me, they probably don't think I'm gay per se, but neither do they think, "That guy is totally overdoing it in the cheeseball macho department, like maybe he's secretly gay or something." I don't mean that they would never *not* think I was secretly gay. If they did or didn't, it wouldn't surprise or offend me. Neither would be a biggie. Because it's not like I'm super-concerned about the opposite of whatever that is.

Jottings from my Moleskine

The blind African-American governor of New York—the way he walks. Charges straight ahead. No tap-tapping cane for him. He trusts his aids, a crew of Caucasian men in ties. Don't we all have the equivalent of that necktied crew inside us? Learning to trust the self. Learning to trust the crew—that's called leadership. But how did I originally think this related to the self?

Put at top of next week's Ponder List.

I was walking down the street the other day when a man in a wheelchair asked me to open a door for him. (Of course if he hadn't asked, I wouldn't have assumed he needed my help.) Then I noticed it was the door to Starbucks! Now I don't know whether I should feel good about helping someone or bad because I indirectly added to the coffers of corporate coffee.

BEVERLY GUILT-BILLY

Dear Beverly,

You've already mastered the art of not treating the wheelchair-bound any differently from anyone else. Great! Now extend that thought. Reach and two and reach and four and reach and reach and reach and reach! Where did you end up? Hopefully all the way to your own back pocket, where you've placed a map of independently owned coffee shops. A map you can hand to anyone, regardless of their color, creed, or degree of ableness. Add a few notations with arrows pointing out the special features of each coffee shop. "100% Fair Trade!" for example, or "Super yummy and organic!" Make your arrows do little loops to show your goodwill and jocularity. Casually slip in a few comments especially for your wheelchair friend, like "By the way, they've got a terrific ramp!" and "Now you're rolling!" Next to that last comment, draw a goofy smiley face with its tongue sticking out. This doodle will show you realize we're all muddling through the big crazy game of life as best we can, and that you don't look down on anyone. Even someone who happens to be both paraplegic and in need of a friendly reminder about responsible consumerism.

Jews in December

You probably think your bases are covered in December because you're always careful to use the religiously neutral expression "Happy Holidays."

But if you see a Jewish person and Hanukkah is already over, the proper greeting is actually "Happy Holiday," since only one holiday—New Year's—would apply to them at that point. If you don't know whether Hanukkah is over or not, cover your bases by saying "Happy Holiday(s)." Pronounce the parenthetical "s" by pausing a beat after "holiday" and then hissing one octave lower than your normal speaking voice.

As for how to spell Chanukkah, this is a bit of a moving target.

Just remember that there are many spellings, and whichever one you're using is probably wrong. And please note that some Jews celebrate their own (equally valid!) New Year's in the fall. In January, you should therefore say to them, "Happy First New Year," or "Happy Christocentric New Year." You may find that Jews are sometimes surprised to receive a greeting so much more evolved than they're used to. So surprised that they may be at a loss as to how to respond. But you'll find response enough in the light of gratitude shining in their eyes. Not unlike the sacred light of Hanukkah itself.

As you've correctly noted by now, worrying about non-mainstream holidays is an essential part of Christmas magic. Hanukkah, Kwanzaa, and that Muslim one, whatever it's called—when are they, anyway? They seem to slip disconcertingly around the solid rock that is December 25, falling before Christmas one year, after it the next. They might end as late as January or begin as early as November. They last for a week or so. A little more in some cases, a little less in others. Or is it alternate weekends? These holidays seem to involve candles, presents, and feasts (fasts?).

My recommendation is to buy yourself a holiday(s) present: the JOSEPH CAMPBELL FOLLOW YOUR BLISS CALENDAR. It lays it all out for you. Not just how we're all climbing the same mountain on different paths, but *when*.

After you've memorized the dates of the holidays minorities celebrate, slip references to them into daily conversation for the benefit of your friends. "Well, of course, the traffic is bad," you can say, "what with this being the third day of Kwanzaa and all."

Guilt and the poor

Sometimes the challenge of diversity is not about ethnicity and religion so much as economic position. For example, what should you do when you're visiting a country with a lot of poor people? How can you deal with the guilt? This is a problem that carries a solution within itself—like the prize in a box of Cracker Jacks, or those handmade crafts in your carry-on.

Because what does it mean when you feel guilty? It means you're a good person. And therefore . . . you shouldn't feel guilty! Actually, you should feel better than not guilty. You should feel great, because you're focusing on the most important issue here: your own feelings. After all, you must *be* the change you want to see. Therefore a better world for everyone starts with you.

And unlike most people, you've taken the trouble to travel where developing people live and learn about their culture. Maybe you're checking into an ashram in rural India, or enjoying an eco-tour of Belize. Don't flinch from the crowds in dusty streets. Remember that we're all part of the same crazy Dance of Life. Sure, the dance has sad parts and slow parts. Smile at the indigenous folks as you pass, to show that you accept your part in the dance, and theirs, too.

Productive communication with grocery store workers

Back home, dancing on the edge of this privilege gap requires less global consciousness and more care about where you step. It's not enough to view yourself as being equal to the people who ring up your groceries, foam your milk, and massage your body. You also have to find some way to express this view at every moment of every interaction with them. This is particularly tricky on those occasions when your loud-and-clear egalitarian subtext also contains a complaint.

Like if your grocery store cashier is practically *hurling* your food at the baggers. Spiritually aware individuals know that actions carry energy, and that food in particular can easily be imprinted with careless negative energy. But it won't do to get mad at the cashier for not being a spiritually aware individual. Instead, take a deep breath and reflect on your relative privileges. Not helpful: making judgments. Yes, helpful: offering tactful pointers in terms the cashier can understand.

So rather than confronting the cashier directly, hint at your meaning in a friendly manner. Like the Buddha, who once responded to a disciple's question by silently holding up a flower. Don't be afraid to also *turn on the fun*! Fix the cashier with a goofy smile and say, "Hey, I bet you were a lawn dart champion in a past life!" Then look meaningfully into the distance. The next time you're at the store, seek out the same cashier and offer another comment carefully crafted to lead them to a higher level of food sensitivity. Some examples:

- "Ever had your feelings hurt? I know I have. Not very fun, is it? Oh well, you know what they say, You are what you eat!"

- "I bet your unconscious vigor could be harnessed for positive ends. If you know what I mean."

- "Have you ever imagined you were a banana?"

When you think that cashier is making progress, move on to the next one, and repeat the process. It won't be long before the manager will be pulling you aside—to thank you for helping the checkers better understand their jobs.

*

Another sticky situation at the grocery store comes up when they ask, "Do you need some help with your bags?" If you accept, are you exploiting the workers or merely availing yourself of a service you've already paid for with your grocery bill?

If the question leaves you paralyzed with indecision, relax! It's actually OK to let them help, so long as you do the following two to-dos. As with the food-hurling cashier, here, too, to-do number one is to reflect on your privileged position. To-do two: transcend this position. In other words, you may have arrived in the land of Good for You! but this is only a way station on your journey to What Was the Issue Again? Translation: You must learn to converse in a natural manner with the young man carrying your groceries. To show you're as comfortable with him as you are with people in your own income bracket.

But what to talk about? Chances are he's a sports fan. Even if you don't follow sports (I sure don't!), all you have to do is ask how he thinks your hometown team is going to do this year. To strike the right jaunty tone, make up a nickname for the team. If the team is called the "Giants," refer to them as the "Big Guys." You can also throw in a little profanity to show you're a regular person. As in, "How 'bout those fuckin' Big Guys this year, eh?" When you feel the impulse to give him an accompanying playful slug on the arm, then you're really getting into the groove. Don't follow through on the impulse though, as it could cause him to drop your groceries.

Bantering with your barista . . .

You've probably heard the saying "That and a dime will get you a cup of coffee." It dates from an age unburdened with real-time knowledge of the world's great cruelty. These days your laptop is a window into Darfur villages burning on Google Earth, and your latte is the beige bull's-eye of a series of concentric circles of shame. The outermost circle is composed of the misery of the people who pick the beans. The next circle, in this series that will eventually lap onto the shores of your local coffee shop, is described by the trail of pollution left by the planes and trucks that deliver the beans.

Even so, our faith in our own idealism is strong, bolstered by the higher prices we pay and the smiling black and brown faces in those Fair Trade brochures. If this faith crumbles at its edges into sentimentality, isn't that better than not giving a damn? As I put it in a recent poem:

> A certain hope,
> disdained by the cynical,
> in the power of collective action
> burns yet on, burns yet on,
> in my throat now.

But what I want to address here is the innermost circle of shame, your interaction with the stylish-and-yet-no-insurance-having worker who prepares your beverage. The heart of this interaction is the tip, which must be delivered with great delicacy. If the barista at any point thanks you, you've blown it. You want the tip to be noticed, but you don't want it to appear that you want it to be noticed. Drop that dollar in the jar immediately after receiving your change while smiling blankly at a point six inches to the left of your barista's face.

. . . and with your massage therapist

Taking off your clothes in a candlelit room to the sounds of a tropical rain forest? You must be getting a massage! If this is a new experience for you, you may have some questions. Maybe you wonder if it's weird to feel uncomfortable about getting a massage from someone of the opposite sex. Or if it's even weirder to prefer someone of the same sex. And how about chitchat—how much is expected during and after the massage? Should you feel guilty about being able to afford a massage? Can people who give massages afford to get massages? And finally, can you remember the difference between a masseuse and a masseur?

No, you can't. No one can. No one can remember the price of a first-class stamp either. That's why we use two stamps and say "massage therapist." Our mail doesn't come back and we avoid that impossible masseuse/ur swamp. The word "therapist" also extends the proper respect to these highly trained professionals. And you should rest easy about whether their income level puts them in the massagee class or not. We can safely assume they have some kind of exchange arrangement with their fellow therapists.

To relax about all of this, all you need is a little more knowledge. Plus, your therapist will surely appreciate your taking the time to learn about their craft. I personally like to use that pre-massage chitchat to show that I realize there's a whole universe beyond the basic Swedish rubdowns so popular with the masses. "Do you agree," I'll ask, "that the Shiatsu versus Derivative Shiatsu debate is totally missing the virtues of a Qi Gong approach? And what is your position on transverse friction? Is it better than light petrissage or effleurage when treating subcutaneous adipose tissue?"

When the massage itself starts, I like to space out and stare at the anatomical charts. I've always wondered if the color they choose for the muscles on those charts is based on the color of raw beef. Or if that's the real color of muscles for mammals.

Tipping, alternative health care workers, and you

We inhabit a wilderness of Reiki Masters, Healing Touchers, Low Qi Specialists, Rolfers, Dulas, Hydrotherapists, and Orthomolecularists. While some of these alternative practitioners may welcome your tip, others may see it as an affront to the validity of their discipline. Think how your X-ray technician would feel if you tried to tip *her*. This isn't as hard to sort out as you may think, though. Just watch for any of the following signs that your therapists would see a gratuity as gratuitous:

- Their title includes a word of three or more syllables.
- They wear a white lab coat.
- Their job involves human birth.
- Their office is a place of clinical silence rather than softly noodling Celtic harps.

In the absence of these signs, the standard 15 to 20 percent applies, depending on the degree to which your spirit was refreshed.

The differently privileged during the holidays

Perhaps your bus driver is a divorcee trying to keep her three kids out of trouble. Or your office intern is from an at-risk youth program. Does that mean that you can't give them holiday gifts for fear they'll feel awkward in their inability to reciprocate? Not at all. We've already seen how the challenges of greeting Jewish people in December can be surmounted with a little diligence and a willingness to hiss a parenthetical s. Downward giving can be accomplished with equal grace. The key is in choosing the right gift. I recommend a book of Dorothea Lange photos. This will both call out the crass materialism of Christmas and show your sensitivity to the recipient's economic position. The more astute among your recipients may also discern the invisible second part of this gift: the chance to gain a greater appreciation of their own background. "These folks sure do have a sense of quiet dignity, don't they?" you can say while looking at the photos over the recipient's shoulder. "Their eyes—just haunting! This is certainly suggestive to me of how I might deal with poverty in a more spiritual way."

That's called reaching out. Here are a couple more examples in exchanges I had with readers on the other side of that privilege gap:

Duke. Howard. USC. Michigan Law. Do I care where you went to school? No, I do not. And yet here it comes again, that tasteful font across your sweatshirt, spelling out the name of your university.
                                                          HIGH-SCHOOL GRAD

Dear Grad,
     This? Sure, it has the name of my alma mater on it, but that's pretty much an accident. I just threw it on as I was making my way out to jog or pick up a few things at Whole Foods. True, its soft, sun-bleached shapelessness may comfort me as I make my way through the weekend, as if I were enjoying the daylong embrace of a quietly prestigious Muppet. But that's not because I want to trumpet the name

of my school or because I think that my school is better than your school. This sweatshirt is just a spontaneous expression of who I happen to be, a guy who happened to go to this school. The name of which you perhaps have heard, since it's pretty well known. My university sweatshirt is good for more than just casual Saturday afternoons, by the way. I can match it with a pair of sport sandals and I'm ready to hit the opera.

The MacArthur Foundation supports creative people and institutions committed to building a more just, verdant, and peaceful world. "Verdant"?

RADIO RAHEEM

Dear Raheem,

Do you feel somehow excluded by that word? Do you find that it falls with an uncolloquial thud? Cast off the anti-intellectualism of your own ears. Get comfortable with this perfectly good word by using it at least ten times every day. "What a verdant salad," you can, for example, exclaim, "it has ever such a myriad of lettuces!" Keep this up until the word sounds as natural as your own breathing. The idea is to soften that thud. Soften and sweeten it until it rings with the delicate tinkling heard by the veteran NPR listener, who accepts such words with a literate nonchalance.

Besides, what other word could you substitute? "Lush"? That's a tad frivolous for the serious business of saving the environment, don't you think? It smacks of sensual pleasure. "Fertile"? Well, OK, I guess. But that has certain associations with human reproduction. Now, I know some people choose to have children instead of dogs, and I find that perfectly valid. There's nothing at all weird about having a child. Especially if you have only one—that's a pretty tasteful number of offspring. Of course some people have more than one child. Maybe even as many as three. Three does seem like some kind of limit though. Beyond that and, no offense, you're liable to seem a bit on the verdant side.

Now here's an example of someone who needed a gentle lesson in this gentle art of reaching down:

While visiting your city from New York, I couldn't help noticing that you all seem remarkably willing to engage in conversation with random crazy people. Where I'm from, if someone comes up and tries to talk about how Sarah Palin is going to lead a pitchfork-wielding army of fetuses against Barack's Washington, the proper response is to avoid eye contact and move away quickly.

But here I heard one woman say to a man in soiled pants and a ripped jacket, "Well, anyway, at least it's Friday!" As if on the weekend he would be relaxing from a long week of scrounging for cigarette butts by scrounging for cigarette butts in a more leisurely manner. Do you see every interaction with street people as some kind of test of your tolerance?

CRUD SHUNNER

Dear Crud Shunner,

If it seems like there's some kind of test, that's because there is. You've heard of secret shoppers who are hired to check a store's service? Well, in this city we have secret street people. They'll note not just overt rudeness, but also the waves of superiority you may emanate while standing at the bus stop like an imperious radio tower. Is that man in the alley ranting at God or relaying a report on your attitude via a Bluetooth device implanted in his skull? You'll never know.

But don't worry! Talking to them is not as hard as you might think. Most every conversation—with a crazy person or not—follows a pattern we can grasp without conscious thought. Simply relax and let the pattern assert itself like the moon on the ocean tides: Someone makes an observation, then you make sounds of agreement. So if a man in a soiled

Marlboro cap turns his bloodshots on you and observes, "Mother Squirrel's pissed a right fortknock ruddy," smile brightly and say, "Fortknock ruddy indeed!" See? It's all in the rhythm of the thing.

But perhaps, unable to simply surrender to the gentle, timeless flow of human courtesy, you're doomed to fail the test put to you by the next secret street person you meet. Half a block later, you'll feel yourself being steered by the elbow into the back room of the nearest independently owned coffee shop for a complimentary soy cappuccino and a quick little seminar. Don't panic! You're perfectly free to go. Just as soon as you grasp a few principles of tolerance. You'll emerge blinking out into the street twenty minutes later with a more compassionate view of the downtrodden of the world. Even if you *don't* have a run-in with a secret street person, perhaps you'll spontaneously realize that mocking the weak is not the most productive use of your energy.

Tag, you're it! Passing along the diverse word

So how will you pass on any unlikely bits of wisdom we may have rustled up here? I think you'll find that the most unlikely of situations will present opportunities. For example, say you notice a co-worker has returned from the bathroom with a streamer of toilet paper sticking out of her pants. What to do? Traditional cultures are full of folktales that empower women, so why not make this an occasion of lore transmission?

Casually sidle over to her cube and say, "You know, [co-worker's name], there's a wonderful story told by the Mayans about two old women who lived together. You see, Mayans had a much more tolerant view of elderly lesbians than we do. It was just no big deal to them. One day, one of these Mayan lesbians saw a bird struggling to free itself from a trap. Murmuring soothing words, she freed the bird, and continued on her way, thinking nothing more of it. That night the bird came to her in a dream. 'Because you were so kind, I have granted you a tail,' said the bird. 'You can use it to carry your water bucket and sweep out your quaint stone foyer. And,' continued the bird with a wink, 'do whatever else you might want to do with a tail.' In the morning the old woman was amazed to find that she really *had* grown a tail. A long, sturdy one. Her life partner mistook the tail for a poisonous snake and chopped it off with a golden ax. That's when the old woman finally came to value herself as a complete and whole person, even without a tail. Now, whether this was some kind of phallic symbol or not," you can conclude while glancing with a friendly grin at the toilet paper coming out of your co-worker's pants, "it kind of reminds me of a little something *you've* picked up, [co-worker's name]."

Then you can both enjoy a good laugh. You're bound to win mucho points for humor and tact. It will only be later, when she has a quiet moment to reflect on the story of the Mayan lesbians, that your co-worker will also come to be grateful to you for the little dose of folk tolerance that you sneaked in.

And—oops!—don't look now, but I think that's exactly what we just sneaked in with this chapter. Huh! How about that?

Transportation

From A to B, conscientiously

Are you doing more damage to the environment than your fellow commuters, or less? Public transportation, for example, is better than driving, but is it better than walking? How about owning an electric car—better than riding the bus? I admit it's confusing. There is one key to understanding it all though: the Hierarchy of Transportation Righteousness.

The lowest point in the Hierarchy is the very fuel-inefficient steamroller. One step up from steamrollers are Hummers. The less said about the remaining few deluded souls who drive those things, the better. One *very* small step up from Hummers are SUVs. Then, in ascending order, there are minivans, station wagons, compact American cars, compact Japanese cars, and compact German cars, followed by biodiesel, hybrid, and electric cars. That covers the car basics, but there are details, exceptions, and subtleties. A battered old Volvo, for example, scores high enough on the Soulfulness Quotient that it easily outranks a cleaner-running but bland Honda Accord. Also, ruggedness counts. Some vehicles get by on a woodsy aura. No, not that 4x4 SUV. I mean the far more authentic Jeep sitting ten spots above it.

Above cars, there's riding the bus sitting down, riding the bus standing up, using a wheelchair (electric), walking, walking with a child, using a wheelchair (manually powered), and walking while pushing someone else in a wheelchair. Riding a bicycle is better than all types of walking because it represents an alternative transportation paradigm. Pulling a child in a Hurley rates above solo riding. Biking with a dog on a leash can move you up or down, depending on the well-being of the dog: up if the dog is fully engaged in the process, down if he's panting and fearful.

But if bikes are tops, what's tops for bikes? That would be the recumbent bike. It sits high atop the Hierarchy, a guiding light, humble and twinkly. My own recumbent bike is constructed of reclaimed military hardware and sports the distinctive lumpy brown hemp tires made by one of those guys down in Portland. I may smile up at you as I glide by your ankles. My smile says, "Waiting for the bus, eh? Consider a recumbent bike! OK, have a great one!"

But for now, please grab a handrail, because your current mode of transportation is the high-speed glass elevator in which we'll tour the Hierarchy.

Starting at the very bottom:

Cars

They're undoubtedly a force for evil, yet some of us are stuck with cars. Purely out of necessity. I myself have a Prius I purchased with the money from the sale of my Subaru Legacy to a Somali family. I think they appreciated that the car came with a free "Co-EXIST" bumper sticker.

I'm sure they could tell they were dealing with a tolerant person when they happened to arrive at my house just as I was finishing my tai chi routine in the front yard and I greeted them with a little ceremonial bow.

I like to think of them out there in my Subaru somewhere, maybe taking the kids out for ice cream. They must know me a lot better now, having explored my radio presets. What a surprise they'll be in for when they go from NPR to "Layla" in just two buttons! Then they'll know I'm a guy who's not afraid to mix a little thinkin' with a little rockin'. Maybe they'll even come by my house sometime just to say hi. That would be a surprise, but I'd do my best to welcome them. Maybe I could reprise my famous tai chi bow and we could share a laugh.

I'm afraid trading up to a Prius is out of the question for every-one else though. Because if you sell your current car and get another one, there will then be two cars where there had been one. Far from shrinking your footprint, you'll be expanding it like a menacing shadow across the land. I didn't realize this myself until after I was already enjoying my Prius's surprisingly zippy handling and astonishing fuel efficiency, secure in the knowledge that my stodgy old Subaru had been honorably pressed into the service of a hardworking immigrant family. I've also moved up a level of subtlety in the bumper sticker department. The one I have now says, "The means matter." What does that mean, you ask? Think you might want to ponder that yourself for a little while? Your shy smile tells me we now both know we're getting into so-crazy-it-just-might-work territory with *that* idea.

So congratulations, now you're a real woman. Or a man. You could be a real woman or a real man, but the point is you're real. Just like the people we're going to hear from in a little bit. They're real, and so are their transportation questions.

First though, I've got to let you in on some secrets that you may find shocking. Shockingly thoughtful, that is!

Confessions of a pedestrianphile

I may have a car, but I use it for essential services only. I plan to mulch it the moment this city deigns to provide wild salmon at a reasonable price within walking distance of my town home. So I'm not, strictly speaking, a "driver" even if I do occasionally "drive" in the technical sense of the word.

And on those rare occasions of "driving," I have the opportunity to interact with the pedestrians with whom I share the surface streets. These interactions mean a lot to me. If I see you out walking, I'll be more than excited to let you cross. Even if there are five miles of empty road behind me, and it would be easier for both of us if I just kept going. Because the issues here are bigger than that. "Congratulations on your progressive use of walking as a form of transportation," says my smile, half glimpsed behind the sky reflected on my windshield. "I'm right there walking with you, my little walking friend, if only in spirit. No need to thank me, just hurry along. My engine is gonna have to switch back to gas here if you don't hurry! Every moment you hesitate only makes it worse!"

The way some people drive

Your interactions with other drivers offer another opportunity for you to let your thoughtfulness shine, shine, shine. Say you and another car come to a four-way stop at the same time. There is no real rule for this situation, but there is an underlying principle: The more considerate person is right, and the less considerate person is wrong. If the more considerate driver is you, you should smile and graciously wave the other car past. There may be some back-and-forth while the other driver attempts to establish the dominance of their own generosity. This may go on for a while as you and the other driver simultaneously wave, lurch forward, stop, and then wave each other forward again. Stick with it though, if you're really sure you have what it takes to outlast the other guy.

A word of caution though. Don't overindulge in the feeling produced by the begrudging wave of thanks from the other driver. It's possible to actually become addicted to the hands of strangers silhouetted in windshields. This condition is known as Wave Hoarding, which is a kind of Karma Hogging. Victims of this condition fear the day that they'll have to return a wave and thus lose a unit from their shadowy stash. If you become afflicted, don't worry. It's fully reversible. Decisively seize the right-of-way occasionally. This will keep you alert and humble.

Life cycles, traffic circles

The oppressively masculine right angles of the four-way stop may become a thing of the past anyway, as they're gradually replaced by the gently flowing curves of the traffic circle.

I've heard complaints that they're inconvenient. Well, traffic circles are many things. They're brave oases of nature in a desert of pavement. They're inspired by European theories of traffic flow. They're utopian havens of communal gardening. (Though some communal gardeners apparently need to be reminded about traffic circle no-nos, so let's go over the list again: nonorganic fertilizer, nonnative plant species, and bake sale notices. I know it's for your kid's school, but it still represents a commercializing of public space.) But inconvenient is one thing they're not. If anything, they should try to be *more* inconvenient. There are people who don't yet feel sufficiently admonished for using the streets for driving. That's why some neighborhoods are experimenting with traffic bio-swells, traffic battlements, and traffic moats.

Sometimes East Coasters who haven't quite caught on to the new spirit of driving wash up on the shores of my column. We're going to meet one of them now. See? I told you we'd get to the real people eventually. And let me tell you, this next letter writer turns up the "real" real loud! We're not quite accustomed to her style of communication here, but her spirit is surely something to admire. Don't trust a man who doesn't appreciate a spirited woman, that's what my dad always said. He didn't, actually. He didn't really tell me a whole lot of anything. But that's OK, because I've had a pretty good time making up imaginary sayings of his. Dad Quotes, I call them. There's a whole notebook of them in my closet somewhere. Moral of the story: I turned this woman's fierce realness to more positive ends with a dose of my patented friendly teasing.

Why can't you people fucking drive? News flash: Your tires are made of high-tech rubber. A little drizzle isn't going to make them slide off the road. I learned to drive while negotiating tractor trailers, grandma-driven Chryslers, UPS vans, and BMW yuppies, all of them cutting each other off on the Brooklyn-Queens Expressway, and to me it's like your roads are clogged with impossibly slow, dumb animals. I could go on, but I recognize your time is valuable, and I'm sure you have a new package from Netflix to attend to.

BROOKLYN BABE

Dear Babe,

Whoa there, Ms. Grumpy Pants! Did someone get up on the wrong side of the buckwheat pillow? Hey, that's OK.

A quick word about compact cars

Perhaps you've been confused by all those Jeeps and wagons parked in "Compact Only" spots. Well, what is a compact car anyway? A car that I'm driving. And a non-compact car? A car that you're driving. Park in a compact-only spot and you can expect a stern glance from me. Dislodge it from your back and decode it at your leisure. While doing so, please also remember that if I park in that same spot in a Subaru Legacy, the words "Compact Only" are obscured and therefore not applicable.

Seem unfair? Not once you understand the history. Back in the seventies, driving one of the original generation of Japanese compacts was the mark of a progressive, cosmopolitan mind that dared to defy the jingoistic call to "Buy American." They might have laughed at our "toy cars," but we were saving money and the planet.

The joke was on them as our sensible little CVCC engines buzzed past overheated Mercury Bobcats strewn along the sides of the nation's roads. Even as the years brought us progressively larger and more comfortable Japanese cars, we retained our identities as compact-car drivers. Pollution produced by an Acura TL is canceled out by the bumper sticker that says, "Hey, you on the bike! Thanks." Indeed, it has become clear that "compact" refers not to the car but to the mind-set of the driver. In honor of our forward-thinking ways, there are spots in every garage reserved just for us. If you have to stop and wonder if you're allowed to park there, you're not.

I get a little case of the crankies from time to time, too. But please remember that when you come here, you're in the "Safe Place." Would you like to have a productive conversation in the Safe Place? I bet you would. So let's just check our hostility at the door, OK? In fact, if you try, I bet you can set aside strong feelings altogether.

Now that we've gotten that out of the way, let's go ahead and talk about those wild accusations of yours. To achieve a greater harmony with Seattle traffic—and isn't that what you really want?—I suggest you first take a deep, calming breath before you turn the key in the ignition. When you've slowed down your mind, you'll see it's perfectly OK to drive five miles an hour and hesitate at each intersection while trying to decide whether or not to turn. You're actually doing the drivers behind you a favor by enforcing a more meditative pace. Let go and let slow, Babe. Feel our rhythm. Feel the sweetness of surrendering to it.

Taking it public

We're now ready to leave cars behind and ascend to the next level in the Hierarchy, public transportation. But uh-oh! It looks like you've forgotten your bus pass. You have two choices here: explain the situation to the driver or pay the fare. But the best approach is a mushy blend. Neither one nor the other. An edgy vagueness that poisons the air of all within hearing distance. Harsh? Not really. There's just no other way to handle the situation.

So take your money out very s-l-o-w-l-y and say, "I have a bus pass, but I don't have it with me, so . . ." Then trail off and smile tensely. If the driver waves you through, then hooray! You've just earned a free ride! If the driver doesn't stop you from paying, then hooray! You've just earned the right to jam cash in the box and storm down the aisle, frowning at the floor and shaking your head with righteously bottled-up indignation. A buzz of exhilarating irritation will propel you like a rocket through your morning, and be well worth even a peak-hour two-zone fare.

It feels good to be right, doesn't it? But now that you're on the bus, you have to consider the calculus of seat selection. No, your eyes didn't deceive you. I did in fact just say "the calculus of seat selection." I hope my offbeat way of referring to things doesn't throw you off. I'm a *New York Times* reader, so I appreciate dry little touches of language like that. Maybe you think prefixing "the calculus of" adds nothing to the words "seat selection" in that particular sentence. Well, an appreciation for the droll music of words is a gift that seems to be granted with an almost whimsical capriciousness. (Or—and I just thought of this—perhaps a capricious whimsy?) So don't feel bad if you didn't happen to have my luck in this regard.

So anyway, choosing a seat involves a grammar of seat choosery that can be dauntingly intricate. Is there more than one seat open? Morning commute or evening? Are you male or female? What about the person next to you? I'm afraid that without a complete set of data, I am unable to advise you on the proper-syntax-of-seat–selection-behavior thing.

Of course there's another side to the story, another edge to the blade, an innie to this outie. Because on some other day *you* may be the one who sits down first and is sized up as a potential seatmate by random strangers picking their way warily down the aisle.

Jottings from my Moleskine

This thought gave me a silent little chuckle on the bus: Wouldn't these people be surprised if they knew I'm on day 22 of my complete media fast? And that I don't even miss all the bad news? If only they knew how liberating it is. Be patient with them. That's what I tell myself. Don't go too, uh . . . fast? OK, make that *two* chuckles!

In my case, if there's an interesting-looking woman coming down that aisle, I try to smile in a vague manner. Vague because I don't want to make out like my smile is some kind of invitation or something. That would be pushy. Instead I jam my North Face backpack against my knees to keep the seat next to me clear and wait for her to see me as a nonthreatening choice. A quiet garden, as it were. An asylum of courteousness. A safe haven in a world that seeks to objectify her.

Am I being overeager? That in itself could be construed as a species of male threat. Maybe I should stare thoughtfully out the window instead of smiling at her. Slump a little. Be casual. I could even let my backpack encroach a little on the open seat, so I'd have to move it if she starts to sit down. Like I don't really care if she sits down or not. Or make a show of my *New Yorker,* so she knows I'm not some ignorant salesman type who's going to hit on her or something. I could also casually make a few notes in my Moleskine to silently give her the message: Thinker On Board. Above all, I want to make it clear that if she sits with me, one thing I will never, ever do is talk to her.

Shared space, stranger space, your space

Sometimes it's not an interesting-looking woman who sits next to you, it's someone with a distinct lack of respect for the delicate bubble of your personal space. Sometimes you may feel the contours of his body unpleasantly abutting the contours of your body, or suffer the encroachment of their newspaper into your facial zone.

You can reclaim your space without being rude, though it will require a persistent and stealthy campaign. When the next bump tosses your neighbor slightly out of his seat, gently but firmly scooch over and reclaim a few turquoise centimeters of municipal vinyl. (In articulated buses this works best in the bouncy second segment of the coach.) After a few such maneuvers have won you the ground game, it's time to go after your airspace. Pretend you're about to stretch out in a wide yawning gesture. This will make him flinch a little and withdraw his left elbow slightly from its place above your lap. That's when you abandon your yawning feint and with your right forearm deftly take possession of the space he's just vacated.

Try to make these actions seem as natural and spontaneous as possible. If he does shoot you a questioning look, offer up a goofy smile as if to say, "Isn't it funny how you didn't even notice you were in my space?" If you find that your skillful scooching and feinting have won you not only all your own space but some of his as well, magnanimously restore his to him. Taking more than your fair share of territory is the first step toward colonialism.

*

The space inside a bus is indeed a minefield of wordless negotiations and unwritten rules. It might help to master it if we hear some of the specific problems my readers have had. If at the end of the discussion we have more questions than answers, then let's party! Because we must be doing something right!

> *My friend told me this story. She's sitting next to some guy on the bus. She's got the window seat, he's got the aisle. She makes a move to get up, but instead of moving, the guy tries to start a conversation. Is she getting off at the next stop? Well, he's getting off at that stop, too, so she might as well wait and they can get up at the same time. Does she work in the neighborhood? My friend had to practically pummel the guy to get him out of the way. Was she overreacting?*
>
> SOUTHSIDE SUE

Dear Sue,

The rules governing riding the bus are clearer in some cases than others. What, for example, are the rights of people forced to stand when the bus is full? The heart of their dilemma is not discomfort but lack of sovereignty. Get a seat and it's yours for the duration of the ride, but standers are expected to keep moving, a band of dirty hobos pushed ever farther toward the back of the bus. Observe how they look around uneasily when the driver instructs them to move back yet again. Are they in full compliance? Have they moved back as far as possible? If there's any room behind them, they must immediately surrender their current handhold and stagger to the next available length of railing or hand strap. But what if a stander finds a refuge outside the flow of traffic, such as on the steps of the rear door? Can this stander lay claim to the space, or must they continue to be shooed along with the rest of the herd?

Do I pretend to have an answer? No, I don't. Why did I bring it up at all? Because the case you describe, by contrast, couldn't be more clear. It's the most immutable passage in the entire unwritten law book: "When a person by the window indicates they want to get up, the person on the aisle must immediately let them." Indeed, the slightest delay verges on unlawful imprisonment. You as the aisle person must be sensitive to the slightest rustling. If a window person so much as tightens her grip on her backpack, you must lean forward to signal a willingness to spring to your feet if this turns out to mean she wants to get up. But don't get up too early. You don't want to make the window-side sitter rise before she actually wants to. Find the rhythm of her movements. Shift when she shifts. Twitch when she twitches. Make yourself a puppet of her needs. If you manage to step aside with smooth courtesy at precisely the right moment, you may even be rewarded with a pursed-lipped little smile of thanks from the window-side person.

I'm not saying you yourself need to be a better aisle person, Sue. I'm saying that friend of yours would have been well within her rights to pummel that guy who wouldn't let her out.

Jottings from my Moleskine

When I have to stand up on the bus, it's fun to pretend like I'm surfing. The pleasure of bus surfing also reminds me to be thankful for a functioning sense of balance. Gratitude = Balance. Would that make a good T-shirt? Find out if it's taken. Could be our ticket out of this place, Kimosabe!

Say you're sitting on the bus, minding your own business, when the super-creepy-looking guy sitting across from you whips out a huge drawing board and starts obviously drawing you. In my opinion, there are three ways to respond to this situation: Pretend you don't notice and gaze off into the distance; ask why he's drawing you; or tell him to stop drawing you. Which is the appropriate one? Say the guy looks like he's mentally disabled and you don't want to hurt his feelings, but his bizarre behavior is making you uncomfortable. Say the bus is packed and you can't simply move to another seat.

BECKY IN BALLARD

Dear Becky,

Move to another seat. Oh wait, you took that off the table at the last minute. You also added the bit about the mental disability. Is this a setup? Madam, if it wasn't for the sterling reputation of this establishment, I'd be tempted to think that this here game is rigged. All available options on the wheel seem equally unpleasant. But sometimes what the table needs is a bump of the hip to get the ball to fall into the slot of an option heretofore unnoticed.

In your case it's an option that will stop the artist across the aisle without hurting his feelings. You don't even have to talk to him. Just start bobbing your head to make it harder to draw you. If he starts bobbing along to create a state of relative stillness between your heads, initiate more advanced evasive maneuvers. Alternate shaking and nodding motions while mouthing the alphabet and blinking. Throw in a grimace or shrug at irregular intervals. When you arrive at your stop, bob and weave your way to the door, squinting and making a bubble-blowing fish face to keep him from getting a clear look at you.

A lot of work? Maybe so, but in framing the question the way you did, you bought both the casino and its crooked wheel, too.

But remember when I mentioned the *New Yorker* a minute ago?

Because that reminded me of a little note I have here in my Moleskine: "Talk to them about what to read on the bus."

The *Economist*, *Harper's*, *The Kite Runner*, Malcolm Gladwell, Naomi Klein—all impeccable choices. Harry Potter is OK if you don't mind being taken for an amateur. David Sedaris? Passable, but may earn knowing looks from the same group of us who shake our heads at those still reading Tom Robbins and Kurt Vonnegut. "Ah, college," we think, as we settle back into our Cormac McCarthy and Annie Proulx. Peek over our shoulders and you're liable to be swallowed by a mist of evocative prose about mythical cowboys: "Moving like a ginger lynx in the springtime forest all waggle tongued and tobacco speckled and feeling full-on the nagging mass under the sun of his bones within him."

If, on the other hand, you're in the tech industry, *C++ in a Nutshell* is pretty unassailable, though you may risk being outclassed by some guy across the aisle fondling the massive slab of his *Standard C++ IOStreams and Locales: Advanced Programmer's Guide and Reference*.

Jottings from my Moleskine

Haven't read my book club book. Some more general topics to steer tonight's discussion toward:

- Lore. The importance of. Our disconnection from.
- Culture. How it sets out blinders.
- Stories. How they sustain us.
- Language. The tyranny of.
- Simplifying. Why we all must.
- Cute things my dog does.

Don't have anything to read? The use of an iPod is perfectly acceptable, though it seems vaguely uncouth to cut yourself off from other people, even people who will never talk to you anyway. Some solve the dilemma by taking out one earbud and smiling about sheepishly. There's no shame in sudoku, either, but it's not exactly the same as a crossword, is it? In any case, you'd better bring a pen if you want to hang with the real cruciverbalists. See? It's easy to be as comfortable as anyone else in this silent menagerie.

Oh, and speaking of the *New Yorker*, we've passed the halfway mark on our way to the top of the Hierarchy, and I want to celebrate by presenting you with a little gift: a moment alone with me and the best magazine in the world. It comes in response to this irritated reader:

Semicolons. I just hate those prissy little bastards. Is there any reason for a modern writer to use them, armed as she is with, I don't know, periods, for God's sake? Also: totally sick of writers who always cram in extra crap between em dashes, as if their readers would keel over dead if deprived of even one of their insights.

RILED E. READER

Dear Reader,

What a lovely and unlooked-for bit of serendipity that your rough but vigorously executed piece of correspondence should reach me as I slouch about in my most Modigliani-esque pose, the latest *New Yorker* in hand and the virtues of the semi-colon fresh in my mind. Chief among those virtues is its power to bind together the endless, drolly observed segments that make up the sentences in that peerless periodical, sentences that become delicately extenuated sculptures—chockablock with delightful antique proprieties such as the retention of the umlaut in coöperation—rising high into the crisp air of our solemn Northwest attention to their Manhattan pronouncements.

Seriously though, it's amazing that those *New Yorker* guys pretty much knew all there was to know about writing back in 1928 or 1956 or whenever. Always form the possessive singular, avoid apposition when introducing a newly inde-pendent clause, enclose elegant phrases within understated curlicues, etc. I don't know about you, but I practically have *The Elements of Style* memorized.

But, getting back to the task at hand: ferries!

Because not everyone here is from Seattle, I won't go into some of the local topics that have come up in my column. It's a shame to deprive you of these discussions, which can get pretty darn raucous. I'm not ashamed to admit to crying tears of hysterical laughter when we get to joking about where exactly Ballard ends and Crown Hill begins. My commitment to inclusiveness, however, requires that we confine ourselves to subjects of general interest. With this one exception.

Ferries, while they might be characteristic of life in the Pacific Northwest, are freighted with too much insight for us to allow them to sail away without us. So climb aboard the gently undulating deck of the 7:05 from Bainbridge Island and hearken to a pair of tales about everyday conflict:

I commute by ferry and there's something that bothers me almost every morning. People line up on the right side of the walkway when waiting to board the ferry, and keep the left side clear for exiting passengers. But lots of people go up this left lane and saunter up to the front of the line. OK, so it's not exactly breaking news that there are assholes in the world. But what I don't understand is why, day after day, everyone in line ignores this behavior. Do they like being taken advantage of? The one time I said something to a left-lane saunterer, he completely blew me off. When I turned back, everyone in line was staring at me like I'm the asshole. What gives?

SOLITARY LINE MONITOR

Dear Monitor,

Those people aren't following the rules. How does that make you feel? Not very good, huh? I can almost see it myself, the little cartoon rain cloud forming over your head. Don't let that cloud follow you around all day like an orphan puppy. Ride the wave of irritation rising in your chest like a surfer toward a golden future. Feel your balance. Feels good, doesn't it?

I mean, sure, you could continue to directly confront those exit-lane saunterers. But hasn't that already been proven ineffective? And isn't that the very definition of insanity, continuing to do something even after you know it doesn't work? I'm not really saying you're crazy. That you're ready to be strapped in a straitjacket, pumped full of drugs, locked in a padded cell, and force-fed lime Jell-O for the next three decades or so. But maybe that's just what those people think, that crowd staring at you, their eyes like cruel darts in your soul. Like you're a stranger in an evil village.

Hope that helps!

I'm a ferry commuter. Every Friday, during the evening rush, I find that the other passengers spread out over all available surfaces with

their laptops, bike shit, backpacks, luggage, and sundry other gear.
Everyone ignores me standing there without a seat. How can I make
a stand, er, sit against these selfish sprawlers?

IN BAD STANDING

Dear Bad Standing,

We're an introspective lot around here. It accounts for
what some see as a glassy-eyed look, and what causes us
to perform certain everyday functions in a distracted manner. Such as when we stand in the doorway of a busy store
to check our phone messages. But I say to everyone stuck
behind us, would it really kill you to slow down a little and
just *breathe*? We're doing nothing more harmful than contemplating our inner landscapes. Our phones are irresist-
ibly fascinating windows into these landscapes. Indeed, it's
arrogant to insist on the primacy of physical "reality" in the
first place. Who's to say Jung's Oversoul can't be found in
the cloud of wireless data humming all around us?

Here's how this relates to your problem, Bad Standing.
You see, sometimes this Northwest self-absorption reaches
the point of total self-saturation. Like a muddy hill in the
rainy season. That's when a person's self bursts the boundaries of his (or her) body, filling and expanding his (or her)
bubble of personal space. This bubble, which normally con-
tracts in crowded conditions, can at these times easily fill
one of those oversized ferry booths. Even at rush hour, with
you standing plaintively nearby, Bad Standing.

The good news is that you, too, can sink contentedly
into yourself. Sit down on the floor. Stretch out your legs
and your own bubble of personal space. Open your laptop,
fan out some papers in front of you, and stare at your phone.
Make yourself so comfortable you don't notice that you're
blocking in one of those booth squatters.

Walkin'!

We're really making some progress up the Hierarchy now. After all those tense, silent interactions with strangers, isn't it a relief to be alone with your own two feet and fall into that left-right-left-right rhythm of the bipedal locomotion that is as much a part of being human as opposable thumbs? I really think you're going to enjoy this part. If, that is, you're willing to seriously consider this question: Do you know how to walk?

Well of course you *know* how to walk. But do you, you know, *know*? There are some rules and procedures that may not be obvious to the walking layman or woman. Not that I'm *not* a walking layman. As I can't emphasize enough, we're all learners here. And all learners benefit from reviewing some basic procedures.

Like the ones that concern the jaywalking of your fellow pedestrians. There's a myth about Seattleites that we're stridently anti-jaywalking. That's about as ridiculous as the idea that we listen to grunge on our houseboats all day while drinking Starbucks. True, maybe when we're waiting for the light we're not seized by such hysterical impatience that we're impelled to take a half step off the curb so we're practically standing in the traffic. Like they do in Manhattan, for example. We're not judgmental about it though, as if we think the unexamined frenzy of those New Yorkers renders their lives somewhat less meaningful than ours.

But even here, in supposed stickler Seattle, we have a range of responses for when you're waiting for the light to change and some guy next to you suddenly jaywalks, leaving you feeling like a dork for continuing to stand there though there are obviously no cars coming. Sure, just standing there and feeling like a dork is certainly one option, but there are three others.

One: Waiting for the light while looking nobly into the distance and taking no notice of the jaywalker. This is the safest and most popular choice. Two: Jaywalking yourself. You have to do this almost instantaneously if you want to make it look like you happened to have the same idea as him, and are not just a mindless follower. Three: Pretending that the jaywalker has awoken you from a philosophical reverie, and then crossing the street with an air of,

"Huh, wouldja look at that? I guess there aren't any cars coming after all!" This doesn't require the same reaction time as Option Two, but still must be executed within three seconds to make it look plausible. After that, you're pretty much stuck with Option One or Option Dork Feel.

Then there's the issue of who gives way to whom when two parties are approaching each other on the same side of the sidewalk. Hang on, I think I've got a chart for this somewhere. Ah, here it is. OK, first you have to find yourself on the categories listed along the x-axis. These categories include: single person; single person with a dog on his right; single person with a dog on his left; and couple walking with a dog on their left and contentedly purring with warm conversation that lingers mockingly in the ears of all those single people. Now find the person or persons coming toward you on this same list of categories along the y-axis. Who should yield is revealed where your x meets their y.

If both parties are in the same category, the chart will tell you to "Get zany." That means you should both try to get out of each other's way at the same time, then start comically weaving from one side of the sidewalk to the other. Waddle like penguins. Screw your faces up in mock consternation. If you're part of a couple, break out the hand jive routine you've prepared for this occasion. What happens next? That's up to you. You can lead a reader to a moment of disarming silliness, but you can't make him avoid a collision.

We like bike

Congratulations! We've now made our way to the tippy toppest strata of the Hierarchy: bicycles. The first thing to remember about a bike is that it's equal to a car when it's on the road, but can hop on the sidewalk and instantly gain the status of a pedestrian. A really fast pedestrian. Ding, ding! On your left!

A lot of people hop in a panic from side to side when I call out that legally mandated voice signal. They don't know what to do when it's bellowed at them from astride an unseen hunk of metal approaching their backs at twenty-five miles an hour. So let's break

But what about skateboards?

They're emissionless and are a healthy form of exercise, so skateboards should rate right up with bicycles, right? But they don't.

Don't get me wrong. I am totally "down with" the vibrancy of youth culture, especially since the basic template of free-spiritedness and political activism comes from my generation. I think it's great that young people should seek out their own fun variation on this template. At least until I hear the roaring, ka-THUNKing approach of skateboard wheels.

Sure, they aren't polluting, and they seem to be having a good time, but how much of a good time should they really be having? The war on global warming is deadly serious. Bicyclists suit up for the battle in helmets, spandex, wraparound shades, and special shoes. Skateboarders, on the other hand, glide down the street in tattered sneakers and tattoos. What can they possibly be thinking about? Are they laughing at me behind my back? No one likes being laughed at. What music are they listening to? They seem to think they've left people like me behind.

That just shows you the value of not judging people, because in fact I actually do like some of the new sounds. I've got a bumper sticker on my Prius for the local college radio station, and even listen a few times a month. But I have to admit they lose me when they say things like "low-fi trio from Brooklyn." I can't tell if inept playing and recording is part of a "style" or what. Why would anyone make their record sound bad on purpose?

Instead of giving in to negative thoughts though, I'm trying to spread a little sunshine in the form of my own music. I've got this little recording project going. It's not a big deal. Not a "look at me, I'm making an album" deal or something. It's just me and Steve-O. A couple of the other guys from my band, the Cool Uncles, might "sit in." This is a bit of a departure for us since we're usually a cover band. Your basic blues-based rock cannot be improved on, in our humble opinion, and so we generally stick to the classics. Can't-miss stuff like Seger and the Doobies, though we like to throw in a little Jim Croce number when we want to slow things down a little bit. So the material we're working on may sound like old-fashioned stuff to some people, but you've got to be true to what's in here. Besides, when did it become a crime to be melodic and soulful?

Song ideas have come from all over the place. I'd had a gin and tonic on a flight to Denver last month, and was staring out the window, grooving to my headphones, when I got the idea for "Don't You Wanna Rock (On a Plane, On a Plane)?" That's the lead track. Then there's "So This Is Feeling (Centered)," on which we showcase for our soft vocal harmonies, before firing up a classic slow burn on "Good Enough for Your Love." Because variety keeps the ears fresh, we get a little psychedelic with "On a Rain Book Stain," deliver "I've Got My Blue, Blue Eyes on You" with a twang and a wink, and get a serious case of the doo-wops on "The Summer's Last Sunday." "Alley Walkin'" is your basic twelve-bar jam, and gives the guys a chance to stretch out a little. The grand finale, and I think we should start closing our live sets with this one, is "Rock On Rockin'."

I know all of that was a more prolonged peak behind my curtain than I usually grant. I guess I'm feeling good because I got another idea for a song just now. It came to me as we were watching those skateboarders come tearing toward us. It's an old-school R&B number I'm going to call "Maintain, Maintain, You Must Maintain Yo' Lane, Wayne."

it down and sing it out in the form of this easy-to-remember jingle, to the tune of that old Oreo cookie commercial: "On your left, so keep your lane or move yourself now, ever so slightly right." I just sang that out loud and I'm pretty sure it scans OK. Why don't you practice singing it, too, maybe the next time you're in the car? And pass it along to your non-bicyclist friends. Lead little sing-alongs of the jingle when you run into them at the grocery store. Remember, those who worry about looking ridiculous rarely make history. And they definitely don't have any fun!

Perhaps as I blaze recumbently past you'll notice what's clinging to my thighs. No, they're not tights. They're bicycle pants. OK, you got me. They're not *just* bicycle pants. They're Moda Eagle Skins. From Sweden. They repel the rain but still breathe. That's cool, though, if that fact slipped by you. I can guarantee you that the other bicycle guys recognize the tasteful little MES logo on the waistband. I mean, not that that's important. I don't notice logos myself. It's just that when you ride a lot, like I do, your gear is almost a part of you. Some people have an appreciation for it, some don't. It's not a big deal either way.

I know bike pants are kind of informal, and that there is a time to have a little more decorum. That's why if I'm making a run to Trader Joe's or something, I always throw on a pair of shorts over my bicycle pants. My comfy old brown shorts. They're a little on the shapeless side, but they've got soul. I've had them forever. The ol' bike-pants-and-shorts look. It's a casual weekend kind of look, but works great for dining out, too.

Not that I'm pretending to represent all cyclists here. I hope I'm never that presumptuous! Because we are as diverse as the bikes we ride. There are the lean young people with their fixed-gear bikes, for example. Not my cup of chain lube, but I don't judge, even if this crowd does seem to value style over the serious business of saving the earth. Competitive bikers, on the other hand, have plenty of seriousness as they go zipping by me in tight formations of matching spandex. Is it some testosterone-fueled frenzy that impels them to make a contest of an activity that might more profitably be enjoyed in a spirit of fellowship? It's not my place to say. I do like to kid them, though. I say "Hey guys, where's the fire?" or "Wait, don't tell me—white sale at Kmart?" I like to think that I'm giving them a little material for reflection, even if by the time I've finished my sentence they've generally become tiny dots on the horizon. Then of course there are the weekend dads on their thick-framed mountain bikes. I always try to encourage these newbies when I see them. "Consider a lower gear for this incline!" I'll call out as I chug past. I'm not looking for any thanks though.

I should make it clear that I'm not trying to imply that bicyclists have more meaningful lives than those who drive, but biking certainly offers more opportunity for personal reflection. Like when the bridge goes up, and you know you've just hit a red light times ten. A full stop, a whole rest. If this happens to you, relax. Join in the spontaneous camaraderie of your fellow cyclists at the gate as they kid each other about who's going to jump the bridge while it's going up, like in that scene from *Dirty Mary Crazy Larry*. Be sure to notice how everyone gets quiet right before the bridge reaches its highest point, as if called into contemplation of the heavens it silently indicates. Oh, and not to break into your reverie here or anything, but just as an FYI, that isn't actually a drawbridge. It's a double-leaf bascule bridge. Feel free to make a note of that.

Biking offers a lot of teachable moments like the one we just had there. If a driver grants you the right-of-way, for example, you should think carefully about what gesture of thanks is best. There's no need to be limited to a friendly wave. Especially if you want to offer some commentary on the fact that you're on a bicycle and they're in a car. In which case a military salute might convey the right tone of affectionate teasing. Like you're saying, "So nice of you not to run me over, Major Polluter!" If you wanted to push this attitude a little bit, you could sarcastically exaggerate your salute and scowl a little. A full-on Fascist salute might be overplaying your hand. For a more whimsical chastisement, you could blow an imaginary referee's whistle, then glare for a second like you're going to call a penalty before breaking into a grin and giving them the touchdown signal.

In keeping with the affection and wonder my recumbent bike excites, I myself like to hold my nose and make a goofy face like I'm going underwater. It's a fun way to convey the message "People driving, oceans rising!"

Jottings from my Moleskine

The sign at the path around the lake reads, "Left lane for bikers and skaters, right lane for walkers and runners." And so forlornly dost I inquire of thee, Parks Department, whither my pogo stick?

A final thought

But should anyone go anywhere at all? No matter *how* you go, you're going to create more carbon monoxide and otherwise poison the earth. Your existence itself is a burden on the environment. That's something to contemplate as our chapter now crashes through the ceiling of the Hierarchy and up into nothingness.

The Environment

Juggling for Gaia

There are a number of non–environmentally-impactful ways to combine Fair Trade coffee and rough-grain brown sugar. The best is the reusable bamboo swizzle stick. Order one at bambizzler.com. It will arrive in four to six weeks. While waiting for it, avoid situations that may lead to stirring. When you get your Bambizzler, carry it on your person at all times. Lick it clean after each usage and return it to its carrying case. If you somehow wind up in a coffee shop without a Bambizzler, you should ask yourself if you really have to stir. Remind yourself that there are millions of people in the world who must make do every day without stirring.

But if it truly cannot be avoided, there are methods that don't require disposable wooden stirrers or metal spoons. You can, for example, gently toss your coffee in the air and catch it in your cup as it comes down. Some of the coffee might spill on your hand and cause minor burns, but these are not nearly as painful as you might think, especially if you focus on Gaia, our Mother Earth. Try softly chanting, "Gaia, Gaia, Gaia," while performing the operation. Or you can use your own tongue as a stirring device. This may be somewhat uncomfortable at first, and will make it more of a challenge to invoke Gaia.

People around you may find these methods peculiar. Ignore them. But do this in a polite manner, so as not to flaunt your superior environmental consciousness.

Now maybe you're beginning to see that saving the earth truly starts in the smallest ways. Let's explore some of these ways.

Do you have to buy organic?

Food is an intensely personal choice, and one that is at the nexus of complex issues involving science, economics, ethics, and the environment. Not everyone can make the right choice every time. And so you occasionally may find yourself supporting the irradiated Frankenfood spewed out by processing plants a thousand carbon-choked miles away, because it's "all you can afford." No need to get down on yourself for that. It may be an obvious truth that what's bad for you is also bad for the planet, but it's also a large truth, and may be hard to comprehend all at once.

I'm sure you do what you can. You might not have remembered to bring your reusable burlap sacks to the grocery store this time, but I'm sure you usually remember, right? Hey, it's OK, I know we're all busy. I'm busy, you're busy. We're busy. But look at me: I still managed to bring my burlap sacks to the store. I just bet you could, too!

If you have forgotten them, you might think that your only options now are paper or plastic. Not so! There's another one staring you in the face: your own two hands. Ask the bagger to construct a pyramid on your outstretched arms with the larger items on the bottom and the smaller ones on top. If you've got a half dozen or so cans of soup, have him stack them into a radio tower on top of your pyramid. True, you'll have to walk very gingerly, and you won't be able to see where you're going. But if you call out from behind your pyramid of groceries that "this is for the earth," and describe what your car looks like, passers-by will be happy to shout out directions. Another option is to ask the bagger to leave a pair of tunnels in front of your eyes. This may take some engineering skill on his part, but it will help if you suggest that he devise a single tunnel with a box of Grape Nuts as its roof, and cleave it in twain with a fruit roll-up.

OK, great job. Now consider taking it to the next level: juggling your items as you walk out of the store. When your performance catches people's attention, then it's "each one teach one" time. Flash a twinkly smile and chant, "Juggling resources, juggling resources, you know we can't keep juggling resources!"

Master this and you're ready to go up still one *more* level: leaving the store without carrying anything at all. Jam carrots into your sleeves. Apply your mouth to the bulk-honey spigot and suck down a week's supply. Scoop from the granola bin directly into your pants. The store should be fine with this if you explain that you'll pay the difference between your weight when you came in and your weight when you leave. And if you promise not to dishonestly reduce your weight by going to the bathroom between weigh-ins. They won't let you use the restroom anyway.

Raw milk

Hello, my fellow criminal. So glad you could make it. This is the perfect setting to continue our discussion of how to effect positive change through consumer choices: Café Name Withheld, a Sunday afternoon raw-milk speakeasy. We're all here to enjoy the creamy goodness that science and the government want to keep from us. You're one of the many new faces I've seen lately. It's great that more people are waking up to the health-giving properties of unpasteurized milk, no matter how belatedly. Welcome, my friend, to raw milk. Welcome home.

Sadly, I must leave this sunny plateau where we food revolutionaries have made such a cozy little camp, but higher ground beckons. See, when you drink even unpasteurized milk, you're consuming something intended for infant calves. This raises certain troubling associations between cows and mothers. Cows may be OK for you, and I hope they are, but I myself need an upgrade in the animal-mother department. That's why I'm headed to a little boutique farm on Bainbridge Island for my monthly allotment of raw alpaca milk. Alpacas are far more alert and lithe than cows, bringing a lighter spirit to the maternal presence in our food lives. And for some reason their milk has never before been consumed in human history, so the unfamiliar jolt of their DNA in ours delivers great vigor of body and mind.

But I will share one last creamy glass of mammalian bounty with you as we listen together to the stories of a couple of my readers grappling with their own food/earth issues:

Sure, you people are tolerant. Not of dissenting political views but of pretentious one-syllable restaurants. Lark, Tilth, Spruce, Bip, Slarn—there seems to be no end of these places where, instead of a meal, you get little cylinders of stuff to smear on tiny crackers. Their grubby casualness is 100 times more smug than any old-school steak house.

MIFFED 'N' HUNGRY

Dear Miffed,

I was just flipping through the channels while reading your letter. Of course, as you might know, I don't really watch TV. I don't even have one. Just a monitor for foreign DVDs. It does have a Comcast box attached, only because I haven't gotten around to canceling cable. I suppose you could call it a TV in the limited sense that *physically* it functions as a TV. But it doesn't have the *role* of a TV in my house, if you know what I mean. Anyway, the other night I was blowing past the news channels to TNT—or maybe the channel a couple of clicks after that, the one that always shows cheesy old movies—when I came across a military flight instructor saying, "If you blink up there, people? You are in a body bag."

I bring this up because it sums up so nicely the American approach to food: fast and lethal. I'm not saying you're guilty of such an approach, that even as I write this you're unloading, with an earthshaking crash, your overfed body from a hulking SUV onto the pavement of the Olive Garden parking lot for their Never-Ending Festival of Carbs. But your impatience with Yab suggests that, at the very least, you've never been to Europe. Please don't take this as a criticism! You can't help that you haven't been exposed to the leisurely, wine-sipping, walk-everywhere Mediterranean lifestyle that informs these "pretentious" eateries. But your travel-deficit disorder doesn't mean you have to cop an uncool attitude while waiting fifty minutes for your entrée. Instead, check your American expectations of instant gratification at the door. Have another glass of $13 wine and settle into the old-world vibe. Bring back the simple pleasures of food by waiting for it without complaint. Welcome your hunger pains as an occasion to reflect on your own patterns of consumption.

Is it OK to use the carts at Trader Joe's?

THE MOMSTER

Dear Momster,

Trader Joe's! My favorite! You know how they get the prices so low? With the power of smartness. Trader Joe's is where smart people buy smart stuff at smart prices. China? No, I'm pretty sure that Trader Joe's would never sell any food from China containing questionable chemicals. Even if some of it may not be organic in the strict sense of the word, Trader Joe's food has a certain organic vibe. In a pinch, this vibe is an excellent substitute for actual organicness.

OK, now look at the aisles here at TJ's. Notice how narrow they are. Wide, usable aisles may have been OK in the past, but *these* aisles are oriented toward the dawn of a more sensible consumerism.

Now look up from the narrow aisles and consider your fellow shoppers. We've all sized down, too. We match the narrowness of these aisles with the narrowness of our carbon footprints. We're thinking sensible, we're thinking whole earth shopping, we're thinking sustainability. A lot of us bussed here. A lot of us biked here. We pull reusable bags like magic handkerchiefs from under our high-tech rainwear, fill them with garlic naan, and attach them to our bicycles with a special system of magnets, recycling, and SmartSnaps.

Now here you come. Perhaps you arrived in that minivan over there. Perhaps your child is with you. And you want to know if it's OK to use a cart. A cart that takes up half the width of the sustainably sized aisles. Of course it's OK! Why would they have carts if you weren't allowed to use them?

Don't mind me as I try to step lightly around you in my complicated bicycle shoes. The little girl clutching shyly at your arm is not in my way. Not at all. Actually, she sort of is, but no worries. I don't need to get to the wine section right away. It's time for me to go gesture reassuringly through the front window to my dog anyway. Kunio's had a bit of a rough week. I think the Spanish lessons are starting to stress her out. Also, I usually make a couple of circuits around the store anyway—once to cover everything on my list, and once to indulge in impulse buys. I try to limit impulse buys to three. I might make an exception if they're having a special on soy flax clusters or pine nut butter, but otherwise, it's three or less. That might seem extreme, but sorry, I make no apologies for living simply so others may simply live. I like to think of it as more of a fun game than a harsh rule. The point is, I can just go ahead and hit that ol' wine section on Circuit the Second. The Impulse Circuit.

This will be the first time I ever picked up wine during the Impulse Circuit, but it's no big deal. Since you and your child and your full-sized shopping cart seem to be in no hurry to settle on a flavor of Orangutan-O's, I'll just go ahead and break that twenty-five-trip streak I've had going since I instituted the two-circuit system back in May 2007 to accommodate both my child and adult shopping selves. Will I finish my shopping with a slightly off-center psyche? Like I said, not a big deal. I've been meaning to work on my re-centering routine anyway. Bottom line, your cart usage is not a problem at all. Just go on with your bad self. Your bad, cart-using self.

I was shopping at a not-so-local natural food market chain. The woman bagging my groceries commented on my choice of natural bouillon cubes (no MSG, no hydrogenated oils). She said, "You know, I really like this product, but I can't get around the fact that it's flown in from Switzerland." Now, I am used to, and find it quite charming, that our local grocery clerks chitchat with us. But never has my grocery selection been criticized. This doesn't happen where I come from. Who does she think she is? It was even more insulting because my mother happens to be Swiss (by marriage).

WHOLLY PERPLEXED

Dear Wholly,

Is it OK for you to have pride in your tenuous Swiss heritage? Of course! But I don't recommend pushing that angle with the cashier. That would just be playing into her hands. If you had Central American relatives and were buying Fair Trade bananas, that would be different. "Flown in from Guatemala"—that doesn't sound too bad. "Flown in from Switzerland," though, wow. With that phrase, the cashier has really zeroed in on the single most irredeemably shameful fact about those bouillon cubes. She's invoked a trail of pollution in the sky that points like an arrow from the Alps to your guiltily pounding chest. The phrase follows you home and hovers ghoulishly over any pleasure you might take in the delicious, hydrogenation-free bouillon. What once added depth to your spaghetti sauce has been corrupted by the acid taste of environmental destruction. I mean, right? If it didn't bother you, why would you write in at all?

Jottings from my Moleskine

Had one of those never-the-same-river-twice moments today. Save for linked *tanka* project?

Going down the wine aisle at Trader Joe's again;

Going down the wine aisle at Trader Joe's for the very first time.

From bread to books

It's not just food, of course. Where you buy your books also has
implications for the earth. For one small local business dedicated to
recycling though, it may be too late. A beloved neighborhood insti-
tution for decades, the used book store is closing for good today.
The store's venerable calico, Dickens, naps sullenly, as if all too
aware that he'll soon be evicted from his sunny window. Maybe
you choose a steeply discounted art book, ruthlessly pressing your
advantage against the bruised flesh of the owner's fortunes. Don't
feel bad about this for even a moment.

True, maybe the place is going under because people like you
long ago drifted toward Amazon.com, or away from buying books
altogether. You weren't there to see the good-natured mischief that
once twinkled in the eyes of the owner as he offered his patented
commentary on each customer's purchase fade to a look of dull
defeat. But it's this look that he now turns on the oversized book of
Renaissance paintings. The one that was purchased from its original
owner for the optimistic price of $40 only last spring and that you've
now plucked from the makeshift "80% Off" table set up where the
poetry section used to be.

He knows it's only the sign in the store's front window announc-
ing its demise that has reminded you of its once-familiar charms.
The silent glow of fellowship from your fellow readers, the soft clas-
sical music, the funky patchwork of fliers in the entrance offering to
massage you, watch your dog, and teach you guitar. A warm, quiet
embrace of your mind and senses.

That's just one way of looking at it, though. Maybe you prefer to
have your books delivered from the Internet, dragging heavily across
the face of the environment their tails of cardboard, air-puffed plastic and glossy advertisements. I wouldn't presume to tell you that
you're helping to kill the planet with your blind compulsion for
convenience and price. That you've grown deaf to the music of the
names of your city's used book stores that once beckoned you with
a slyly understated sophistication. Magus, Horizon, Twice-Sold
Tales, Left Bank, Epilogue. Perhaps you could make this music into
a soundtrack for your meditation on how these quiet little havens

that once enriched the texture of civic life are fast disappearing forever.

Without these bookstores, into what cozy chamber will you duck on a rainy afternoon? But it's all right. Log on and kill off one of the last sacred spaces left in the city, and do a little bit more damage to the environment to boot. Tip the world ever more relentlessly toward sterility and despair, as it were.

The model home

I'm sure you don't want to do that though. So please step this way to learn more about how you can help the planet by buying things. But would you mind removing your shoes first? This is a model Seattle home, and therefore a shoe-free zone. We'll get to why in a second. In the meantime, did you notice that every surface in here is recycled or sustainable? That the fixtures were reclaimed from a 1970s public school, the counters are made from millions of cubic yards of mashed together newspapers and magazines, and the Fair Trade–certified deck furniture was handcrafted out of Shell oil cans by Ghanese villagers? That, in short, this is a place where clean lines meet a clean conscience?

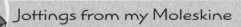

Jottings from my Moleskine

Re-conceptualizing the Northwest winter months.

Morning never comes. The afternoons disappear into a black hole sky. Must think of this period not as day with intervals of night, but perpetual night with occasional surprising appearances by the sun. Flip the kayak of expectations. Paddle upside down in the darkness. The darkness that is my native element now. Surrender to the eerie magic of yellow sodium streetlights reflected on wet pavement. When the sun deigns to appear, must greet it with joy and skepticism. The importance of not becoming attached to the dazzling stream of information it delivers to the eyes with its "light."

That brings us back to why you're standing there in your socks (Oopsy! Someone has a hole!). It might seem like we're just aping a particular Japanese custom. But it's bigger than that. The delicacy of feeling that is the genius of Japanese culture finds its analogue in the delicacy of our carpet fibers. Floors are an investment, and can add or subtract considerably to the resale price of a house or condo. So there are inside/outside, sacred/profane, and clean/unclean implications here. To enter someone's home is to breach the glowing energy field that is its market value. So you must purify your entrance like a sumo wrestler throwing salt, or a Shinto priest waving his folded paper thing around. It's not just carpets, by the way. Those scuff marks on bamboo floors—ugh! Not that they have a lot of bamboo floors in Japan, but there is an evocative connection that floats like a feel-good haze above our tasteful decor. So take off your shoes, close your eyes, and drift off with us into a vague, warm feeling of oneness with nature.

OK, open your eyes! Tour over! You have to go back to your own house now. On your way out, you may notice that there's no welcome mat. Well, we couldn't very well have gotten that kind with an eagle on it. The next thing you know, a Fox News crew would jump out of the bushes, and there'd be a segment about how Seattle liberals hate America so much they wipe their feet on its most sacred symbols. Let them keep hassling San Francisco, that's what I say. And those metal-reinforced coir fiber mats are so brutal and chunky. No, better to go with a no-mat strategy to prepare the way for the no-shoes policy. Let them wipe and they start to get ideas.

Feel free to admire the garden on your way out.

The garden

Readers of gardening literature know that planting a bulb is an act of hope. And that an act of hope is a leap of faith. For there truly is something faithful in acting hopefully, and hopeful in leaping faithfully. Hope. Faith. An act. A leap. Panama! Panama tulips, that is. Plant them now and hope the retired accountant across the street won't show you up again next May. She always has a word of unsolicited advice on how to make your garden bloom like hers. Which is frankly easy for her to say, since she doesn't have to go to work like the rest of us. Your wordless springtime response to her will be the purple profusion of several dozen of these hardy perennials clustered dramatically in a semi-shady area of your yard. Remember not to overfertilize, and your pleasant smile will have the power to silence her from a dozen paces. Good luck!

I know about your other problem, too. That the spinny thing in your garden has stopped spinning. You had some good times watching it, didn't you? "It keeps the birds away, too," you were heard to remark as you happily allowed your tired eyes to be mesmerized by the spinny thing reflecting another summer sunset. We love things, and things don't last. That's the tragedy of human existence.

But ask yourself a difficult question: How much was the spinny thing really fooling your eyes anymore? How much was it fooling anyone's eyes? Sure, for a while it looked for all the world like a magically hovering helix that rotated into existence at its base and upward into nothingness at its top. But you've had it so long that at this point even toddlers and cats turn away yawning.

I suggest you move on to a mobile. That one guy who used to sell sturdy outdoor mobiles made from old cookware and stuff—I think he's still got a stall at the Fremont Sunday Market. Go see him and settle down to a less manic motion over your tomatoes and marigolds. There's no funny business with a mobile. Just a slow, whimsical harmony with evening breezes. Consider it a first step in eliminating deception and spin from your life altogether.

That's not what we were talking about though, was it? Don't worry, I didn't lose my place here. Gardens and their environmental implications. See? I'm on top of it. I do think that we must sometimes make room for a contemplative moment or two though, even in the midst of serious discussions. That's not something I'm prepared to apologize for.

One side effect of having a contemplative bent is that it can be hard to communicate with those who haven't come to the same realizations you have. Here are a couple of green gardeners who learned that there's a time to demur and a time to exploit your advantage:

For the last several months I have been siphoning the gray water out of my bathtub with a hose into buckets and using it to water my vegetable patch. I often have enough extra to toss some water on the lawn as well. I'm saving like mad on my water bill and am proud of my slightly smaller footprint. My problem? As we enter the last days of summer, the neighbors' lawns are all a uniform, righteous, crispy "I wouldn't waste precious water on a patch of lawn" gold, while mine remains conspicuously soft and green. Whenever someone compliments the yard, I of course quickly explain that the water is recycled, but you know how people are with their silent judgments. Do you think it would be too boastful to post a small, tasteful sign on the front gate explaining that I'm not a water-waster? Any other ideas for how I can negotiate this delicate situation?

GREEN GARDENER

Dear Gardener,

Good morning! Your only "problem" is you need to wake up and smell your own freshly brewed strength. Racing down the path of ecological awareness on your commendably teeny, birdlike feet, your mind as sharp as your prose, you've traveled so far ahead of your neighbors that you've come up behind them. So what if they don't realize they've been lapped? Let this fact shine out at full strength from your nimble soul to their numb skulls.

Go ahead with that sign, but not in the meek manner you described. You've got the power, Green, and it's time to make a power move. Grab the biggest Sharpie you can find, flip over that old Obama sign in your garage, and write, "Hey Neighbors! Want to learn how to move beyond your wasteful habits? Want to get a thank-you card from Mother Earth and enjoy a lush new lawn? Join me for a workshop on gray-water recycling. My backyard, 6 a.m., this Sunday."

That's the kind of full frontal assault that'll make you a figure of awe on both sides of your block. Later, it's time for the mop-up operation. When you spot any workshop absentees on the way out to your Prius in the morning, fix them with a friendly grin and say, "Missed you on Sunday!" As you drive away, roll down your window and playfully call out, "gurgle, gurgle, GURgle!" This onomatopoeic stone cast in the pond of your neighbors' minds will bring their own lavish water consumption rippling onto the shore of consciousness.

And I promise, Green, should you invite me to the block party they eventually throw in your honor, I'll make no attempt to usurp your place in the bright center (even if I inspired you in some small, infinitely mysterious way). You'll glimpse me only intermittently, a contented satellite orbiting the farthest ring of your admirers, smiling with quiet pride like Morgan Freeman in *Million Dollar Baby*.

Whenever I go to my local community garden, geezers leap from the weeds with unsolicited advice and insinuations that youngsters like me can't possibly know how to weed or plant. I grew up on a farm. I've gardened my whole life. Is there any way I can shut them down politely without going into my personal bio?

WAYLAID WEEDER

Dear Waylaid,

Well, it's not a contest on who knows more about gardening, is it? I ask this having recently visited a community garden nestled in a quiet corner of a neighborhood of well-kept bungalows festooned with *lungta* ("Tibetan prayer flags" to the Noble Truths–impaired). Stroll through it yourself some summer afternoon, and peace, not competition, will come to dwell in your mind. Sit in the shade of a seventy-foot pine tree and tune your ears to the bugs, the birds, and the breeze blowing through lovingly tended zucchini and hydrangeas. Listen as the sounds of the city fade to an ambient roar against the Cascade Mountains.

But let's pretend for a moment that gardening *is* a contest. Why would you surrender your deadliest weapon? Not your wide-handled Japanese weeding fork, Waylaid. I'm talking about your rural background. Your "personal bio," to use the phrase with which you distastefully push this great asset aside. There's no need to "go into it." Simply brush against its vastness with a show of restraint. "My pa back in Kansas used to say that," you can say when they make their suggestions. "Of course that was twenty years before the farm went totally organic." I guarantee that peace in the garden will once again be yours.

Geese. Their droppings. You.

We're moving outward now, from gardens into the larger cycles of nature. And nature isn't that far away, after all. It's not something "out there," it's all around us, even in the city. In fact—look out!—it's right under your feet. As you just discovered, we've got a lot of geese here in the Northwest. My dog Kunio is allowed to chase them, because he's also part of nature, but some seem to think they also have a license to persecute geese.

There is even an effort afoot to round them up and take them . . . some place. I'm not saying they're being rounded up because of their Canadian-ness per se. And I'm not saying that this is part of a larger hostility toward universal health care and liberal attitudes toward the use of marijuana. Or that the perfection of the fit between the regal necks of the geese and the jackbooted heels of the Fish and Wildlife Service is anything more than a coincidence. All I'm saying is, did we learn nothing from the internment of Japanese Americans in World War II?

Should your neighborhood also be "plagued" with the elegance of these aristocratically waddling waterfowl, I suggest you open your spirit to them. If your path is smeared with their gooey green product, make a game of avoiding it. Goose-step (sorry!) over as many of these blobs as you can. Staring at their whimsical shapes can actually be like cloud gazing. Look, exploding Siamese twin clown heads! It's a game you can get your kids hooked on, too. Or make up some geese haiku as you walk along. Here are a few to get you started. I have kind of a knack for haiku, so don't worry if you can't capture the core essence of the geese quite like this:

> Squishy stepping and
> wry smiles. Our northern friends
> have blessed us amply

> Honk! Honk! Honk! Honk! Honk!
> Music of late Februar-
> y and early March

See? Fun! If there's a problem, it's not on the ground, it's in your attitude.

Is it OK to visit the zoo?

So that's geese. But how about zoo animals? Does visiting them fit with an environmentally conscious lifestyle? To answer that, let me start with the greater scaup, a black-and-white duck who dives for his food. Would he be happier free of his enclosed temperate wetland? Well, on the one hand, if left to his own devices, he could freely roam the lakes and bogs of Europe or North America and otherwise conduct his affairs as any scaup, be he greater or lesser, would prefer to do. But on the other hand, if not a dependent of the zoo, he would be vulnerable to predators and fluctuations in his supply of mollusks and aquatic plants.

Or consider the tapir. Not the star of any animal fable, excluded from the canonic E-I-E-I-O scheme, this prehensile-snouted alternamammal languishes in his pen along the trail through Tropical Asia Forest, ignored by the crowds rushing toward the more mainstream attractions of the Elephant Barn. Is it right that the tapir wanders around aimlessly behind panels of reinforced Plexiglas? Is his freedom worth missing the chance that a budding young environmentalist may have her or his consciousness raised by the informational screen instructing us that this jungle dweller, with his highly flexible proboscis, is in fact an endangered species?

Perhaps my point by now is clear: It may or may not be OK to visit the zoo. The more important thing is that if you *do* go, that you not get so involved with "enjoying yourself" that you miss the many opportunities for self-improving rumination.

Break it to them gently: finessing your eco-vangelism

About now, I hope you're feeling pretty good about yourself. We've learned how every little thing you do is connected with the destruction of the world, and we've had a lot of fun along the way. Now comes the real challenge: how to spread the word to those who aren't quite as far along on their own environmental journeys. These two letter writers learn that teaching moments can be opportunities to create humor unexpected in its efficacy, and art poignant in its ephemerality:

> *There is a woman in my office who brushes her teeth in the bathroom every day after lunch. Problem is, she leaves the water running the whole time. I am a three-minute-shower, rainwater-collecting kind of girl, and seeing her waste water like that drives me crazy, but I don't want to cause undue tension in the office. What would you do in my situation?*
>
> *WATER WISE*

Dear Wise,

What would I do in your situation? Well, if your situation involves the ladies' room, I'm unlikely to be in it, am I? Sorry, I couldn't resist. But did you see how my correction was enclosed in an appealing wrapper of humor, like a prune dipped in chocolate? The bathroom setting you describe suggests how you can find your own humorous chocolate coating for the important message you must convey to this careless co-worker of yours. Why not perform a little lighthearted parody of one of those old teenage-delinquent films? Get a little bit *Blackboard Jungle* on her, but in a fun, girl-on-girl way. Say, "Oh, no, you didn't mean to do that, now, did you, sister?" while firmly grabbing her wrist and fixing her with a stern look. When she realizes she's in a stare-down with you and there's no one around to help, that's when you let her in on the joke. Grin and say, "After all, we girls know all about conservation, now, don't we?" while reaching over and turning off the faucet for her. As the warmth of the campy fun wears off, she will be left with the underlying chill of the initial threat. When she realizes that it's the same threat faced by the earth itself, your work will be done.

Neighborhood guidelines require that my neighbors sign a consent form before I'm allowed to keep chickens in my backyard. Everyone signed except this one woman. What should I do?

CHICK BLICKED

Dear Chick Blicked,

Tick, tick, tick . . . Ding! Time for the ol' eggs-followed-by-origami routine! Deliver to her doorstep a dozen eggs snugly wrapped up in an old-timey picnic basket. A week later deliver another basket, this time containing a dozen delicately folded dodecahedrons. Enclose a note explaining that they represent the dozen million cubic miles of pollution produced by a single carton of eggs on its journey to the supermarket. Faced with such a poetic expression of the cost of not eating locally, she will surely sign your little chicken form.

Kickin' it in the cone

Good work, gang! We've really covered a lot of ground here. I see some of you are already standing up and pushing in your chairs, but if I could have just another moment of your time, there's one more thing I need to share. And this is something you're not going to find in those official brochures by the door. It will help you understand why I do certain things that seem to—what's the word?—"contradict" my progressive beliefs.

For example, you might be surprised to find out I have a leaf blower. "What?!" I can hear you exclaim to each other. "Is this not a machine widely reviled for its appalling noise and air pollution?" Yes, it is. You might also notice a trail of slug poison draining into the gutter in front of my Green Certified town home. OK, OK, calm down, everyone. I know that all *seems* kind of unintuitive, but sometimes we have to make our minds very still to receive a new idea. So if you could stop rustling your coats for a moment and cultivate that stillness, there's a better chance that you'll be able to believe in the magical floating cone I'm going to tell you about. The Cone of Entitlement. Leaf blowers are covered by the Cone of Entitlement, as is wood smoke from my brick fireplaces and the eating of certain endangered fish species.

Because I'm basically a good guy. That's the source of the entitlement. See the name of the company doing my yard? That's right, "Solstice Landscaping." Solstice, as in the rhythms of nature, the dance of the cosmos, a harmony with all that is. See the logo stenciled on the side of the truck, with the pine tree silhouetted against a field of stars? The updraft of warm feelings from this logo suspends the Cone high above the gas-powered pruning equipment.

OK, that's it. Thanks for coming. Now it's time for me to get home to my Kunio.

Doggies!

I once heard a guy on the radio say the reason he always tries to be a good dad is so his kids will have a loving model in their minds when they hear the phrase "heavenly father." Minus the patriarchal trappings, that's how I feel about being a dog caretaker (I don't like the word "owner"). I represent the universe to Kunio, and I want him to regard the universe as a place of love.

Oops! I hope I didn't scare anyone off by getting too deep too soon. I sometimes forget that I've pondered the dog-human nexus more than most people and tend to jump right into the higher principles. We don't want to leave anyone behind though, so let's start with some more specific questions. Starting with the very first one of them all.

Where do dogs come from?

Some people buy dogs from professional breeders. Others adopt rescued dogs. One is not better than the other. True, people who patronize breeders contribute to the problem of dog overpopulation. And the whole transaction becomes just another consumer experience, like picking a brand of cranberry juice. I myself am willing to spend a little extra for the small-batch local stuff that doesn't have corn syrup or other junk added. We as a culture have such a fear of the real taste of cranberries.

Much like customers of breeders have a fear of not getting the exact type, gender, color, size, and disposition of dog they want. Have you ever noticed that the very word "breeder" has an unpleasant look? Type it three times in a row and it looks like roaches marching across the page: breeder, breeder, breeder. Not that *that* means anything in particular. I just happened to think of it, that's all. The important thing is that we all love dogs in our own way.

Of course, adopting a rescued dog means learning how to love on a whole new level. Or rather, learning how to let go and be guided by the light of gratitude shining in your dog's eyes. Follow that light far enough into the warm recesses of your dog's soul and you'll soon begin to wonder who rescued whom. Don't get me wrong. I don't mean that puppy-mill customers don't also love their dogs. It's just that the two experiences are different.

One of the differences is that a lot of dog rescuers have gone to some pretty extraordinary lengths. Sitting on a bench at the off-leash park on a Saturday morning, they'll tell you how they traveled across three states to pick up their bull terrier, who was discovered shivering in the corner by the SWAT team that had just gunned down his drug-dealing, abusive former owner. "Rufus Wainwright still startles easily," they'll say, "and gets anxious around new people. Especially men."

I can sympathize because Kunio suffers from those same effects, which are actually pretty basic for any dog with a difficult past. Kunio's list of aversions happens to be just a little more extensive. It includes hairpieces and circus music. See, he was rescued from a Slovenian carnival in which he was made to wear an orange afro and ride in a tiny car with a lot of other dogs.

I had to travel to Sweden to pick him up. That's where the circus animal rescue agency is—just a *little* farther than "three states away." Who cares though, right? I'm just making conversation here. We were talking about how you should get a new dog and I was simply sharing my own experience. My two cents, as it were.

Training your dog

So now you've got your dog. How do you train it? They always tell you to be in charge with your dog, to be the boss of your dog, to "top" your dog. Haven't you always felt a little bit funny about that? Maybe your dog does need some help focusing on an appropriate agenda for the day. One that doesn't include, for example, attacking the phone whenever it rings. But if there must be a hierarchy, let it be one with softer contours. Instead of a tyrant, be a gentle leader. So gentle that you're not really even a "leader" at all. More like a loving older sibling. A head friend. A fellow creature who just happens to have all the food.

Traditional trainers say packs of dogs in the wild are organized under a single alpha male. But research probably shows that wild dogs have more of a consensus-based society. The "fighting" among dogs is merely a playful celebration of their egalitarianism. Your goal as a steward should be to replicate the classless society of dogs. To create an environment where both human (you) and dog (your dog) are continuously bathed in feelings of well-being. To froth this up into a tasty generalization for you, balance isn't just a product, but also a process. To bake it into a crunchy adage for your dog, Do! Don't do! Good!

Choosing a leash

It's great to see that the message has gotten out about choke collars. I notice when I'm out at the park that most owners have switched to some kind of soft, loose-fitting, non-irritating, extra-wide organic polymer. These good souls are to be commended. Even if they haven't realized they're still focusing all the stress on their dog's throat. Those who have made this realization quickly progress to a harness, one slot up from organic polymer on the Pyramid of Doggie Kindness. Unlike a collar, a harness distributes the pull of the leash across a dog's body. Harness users have achieved a level of empathy that is nothing short of terrific.

So terrific that I'm sure it's only a matter of time before they see the shortcomings of harnesses, which distribute the force more widely than collars, and yet still focus it on a dog's rib cage. Plus, they still involve a leash, which doesn't distribute the force at all on the *human* side of the dog-walking arrangement. A leash has just one point of human contact, i.e., the dog owner's hand. That's why I've devised my own solution, the MultiWeb System. The MWS has *nine* points of contact on the human side, attaching with surgical tubing at the wrists, elbows, knees, crotch, chest, and forehead. Instead of a harness, a form-fitting net of soft plastic sheathes the entire length of Kunio's body and legs. I've found that I can install it on him in about forty-five minutes, depending on his level of squirminess at the time. I leave about seventy minutes to attach it to myself.

Once I have the MultiWeb on, the force is distributed with complete evenness. Rather than yanking Kunio this way and that in a heartlessly linear fashion, I can envelop him in a mist of loving guidance.

Jottings from my Moleskine

The unfunniness of jokes about small dogs. "Size challenged"? The size of people's empathy, perhaps. The ability to ignore the vulnerability shining in those tiny eyes. The pain in their yipping. "Walking mops"? Mopping the floor of their own crushed self-esteem.

Walking with a dog isn't supposed to be some kind of military march with the person as the commander. It should be more like an improvisational dance between human and beast. With the Multi-Web, this dance takes on new dimensions. A lift of my arm may suggest a direction, while an answering pull on my left knee lets me know where Kunio would prefer to go. In response I can pull my head back with gentle firmness, while playfully wiggling my knees to appeal to his sense of the absurd, even as my midsection is pulled forward in sharp counterpoint to this appeal. I've recently discovered that when I want Kunio to go a certain direction, I get good results with my own version of "locking and popping," which delivers waves of crisp little tugs across his body.

I've found the MultiWeb can also subtly transfer body wisdom. When I'm fresh from yoga class and extra mindful of my posture, I find that the resulting gentle upward pull on Kunio's upper torso encourages him to also adopt good posture habits. He keeps me from taking my "instruction" too seriously, though, when he goes charging after a squirrel at the park and I flail behind like a spastic puppet. "OK, boy, OK!" I'll say, tumbling down with a laugh next to him in the grass, "Point taken!"

One bag, two poops

Of course the real goal of walking your dog is defecation. Any conscientious person walking a dog takes along a plastic bag to be ready when the little guy does his business.

But what if you're out for a walk and the dog goes a *second* time? I can sympathize because this happened to me recently. But just as the universe may toss obstacles in our path, it can also, with a mischievous turn of the dharma wheel, offer alternative routes around these obstacles. The trick is to maintain the heightened state of awareness that will allow you to find these playful detours.

My tale begins when I was taking a second lap around Green Lake here in Seattle with Kunio one evening and noticed he was walking in that special, stiff-legged way. My only plastic bag, filled with his first movement, had already been deposited in a receptacle by the boat rental place. Rather than fight nature, I took note of a blessing that was temporarily ours: We were alone in a gap between waves of strollers and Rollerbladers. My voice a careful mixture of urgency and gentleness, I whispered to Kunio, "If you're going to go, go now, boy, *go now*!" His little squinty eyes shining with silent comprehension, Kunio did the deed. I then placed a pinecone on his product, to warn pedestrians, commemorate the special bond between us, and thank the universe for endowing us with the agility to improvise in jazzy counterpoint to . . . But perhaps this is all a bit much for you? If you want advice that's a little more "direct," a little less "nonsensical," perhaps you're not open-minded enough to benefit from my words. Which is fine. Me, I like to find the offbeat, the whimsical, the beauty in everyday life. It's what I do. You, maybe you're perfectly content with a more conventional way of looking at things. Anyway, my story was about a special, onetime dispensation from the universe. Perhaps it's not applicable to you. So just make sure you always carry at least two bags.

Can you leave your dog tied up outside the store?

Sure! So long as you don't mind abandoning him to an ocean of despair. Because there's no such thing as "I'll be right back" for a dog. There's only an eternal now of confusion and anxiety. "Where did the person go?" the dog wonders. "Why did the person leave me here alone? Will the person ever come back?" The dog can only make an eerie whining sound in his throat while staring hopelessly in the direction his person went, as if staring hard enough will enable him to see through store walls.

I know, I know—there are times when even those sensitive to the inner lives of their companion animals must briefly leave them outside a store. There is a solution though. Did you know your dog can be trained to understand hand gestures? Like how shepherds command their dogs from across a field? Develop your own set of signs with your dog. Only instead of imperiously demanding that sheep be rounded up, use your signs to give long-distance emotional reassurance. Rapidly shrugging your shoulders while tapping a fist against your forehead, for instance, can mean "You are loved." Flapping your arms and goose-stepping in place can mean "May all sentient beings be happy—that includes you, buddy! You're a sentient being! You're included in this deal! Yay!" Then, whenever you have to leave your dog outside, simply perform one of these gestures every four minutes through the front window of the store. Proceed with your shopping wrapped in the warm feelings emanating from the wagging tail of your reassured companion on the other side of the glass. Disregard the stares of less enlightened shoppers.

Kunio

I've talked a lot about him here, but please allow me to formally introduce you. Kunio is a petit basset griffon Vendéen, a breed known for their rustic wiry coats and whiskery faces. Yes, he *is* a good-looking fellow, isn't he? He can be willful, but I think that's part of the—Kunio, you stop that barking, you stop it, you big lump of silly! You big silly booger boy you! Who's my sweet bean? Who's my sweetie? You are, you are, YOU ARE! Come gimme kissy kissy wubbby wubby woo boo! You love that, don't you? Oh yes you do! *Oh yes you do!*

Jottings from my Moleskine

Time to eat dog food again? Has Kunio been sufficiently reassured that I would not give him anything that I wouldn't be willing to put in my own body? Check calendar for the last time I performed the Food Respect ritual for him.

Sorry, he's a little wound up from his class this morning, "Worlds Beyond Obedience: Come, Ye Doggies, Gather at the Pool of Wellness." He also had kind of a rough week in doggie day care. The regular woman was out and there was a substitute attendant who—and I feel bad about saying this, because I'm sure she was doing her best—isn't quite as attentive to Kunio's special needs. He needs someone who really "gets" him. So he needed an extra special little dose of love when he got home. Didn't you, boy? Didn't you need a little extra wove when woo wot wome? Oh yes you did! *Oh yes you did!*

Kunio is my walking litmus test. It's very telling how people react to him. He's a Sagittarius like me, so he tends to be on the sociable side, and some people can't seem to go with his goofy ol' doggie flow. Like when he jumps up on them like the big goofball he is, his paws all muddy from his latest adventure. These are the same kind of people that get all freaked out when I bring him into the brew pub or the blood donation center. I've got a note from my therapist documenting his status as an emotional support dog, and I'm totally ready to bust it out. I don't think anyone wants it to come to that.

People allow themselves to be governed by their fears. A lot of it is too much media. You don't watch TV? Well, that's a great start! I myself happen to be in the midst of a complete information fast at the moment, covering not just TV, but all media. So if you bring up some topic, please don't be surprised if I'm unable to discuss it with you. I basically have no idea what's going on right now. I'm convinced that media-driven fear is what keeps people from accepting Kunio as a legitimate member of my family, even though I accept their children as graciously as necessary. Are my good-natured jokes being taken the wrong way, the ones about how a child's impact on the environment is exponentially greater than a dog's, and that there are studies to prove this? Well, what can I do? You can lead a friend to a funhouse mirror, but you can't make him laugh at himself. (I'm going to give it another shot in the next chapter though!)

Some acquaintances of mine are raising their kid to speak Spanish. *"Buen trabajo!"* they always exclaim when he manages to toddle across the floor, and yet they were surprised to find I'd taught Kunio a few Spanish requests. (Kunio and I don't like the word "commands.") And that I assure him at regular intervals that he is *"mi hermoso pequeño frijol."* I want to acclimate my guy's wiry little ears in case we ever run into Mexicans. So he won't be startled by the sound of their language. It's just a little extra trouble that I take with him. To me it's just part of being a good warden. And those Mexicans of the future will surely appreciate meeting such a broad-minded dog. "Well," I'll say with a self-deprecating laugh when they turn in wonder from his furry face to mine, "I only speak *un poco*. I just think it's important for dogs to be familiar with what shifting demographic trends show will be an even more important language in the coming years." The Mexicans may be moved by my humble commitment to non-English-centric canine stewardship, but I'm prepared to wave away their teary thanks. It's just a shame that efforts to close the canine-Spanish gap aren't more routine.

Instructions for the dog sitter

One thing that *is* routine is going out of town and leaving your dog in the care of someone else. Or at least for some people it is. Not for me. Possibly because of my sensitivity to higher truths, I'm unable to take my upcoming separation from Kunio lightly. And—oh my Goddess, look!—only two weeks left and I still haven't worked the bugs out of the preamble to my instructions for the dog sitter. I've got a pile of notes to incorporate, and I'm still tweaking the tone.

Of course, I'll need to appeal to the reader with the title, too, so I've been playing with a few possibilities. "While I'm Gone: Hangin' With Ma Pooch" is friendly, but I want the work to be taken seriously, too. Another contender is "Poop Bags, Vegetable-Protein-Based Doggie Pretzels, and Romping Techniques for Sensitive Paws: The Slightly Crazy and Totally Fun Stuff in Store for You Until I Get Back on the Tenth." It does ring out with the joy that I think is *the* missing component at the heart of interspecies dialogue. But again, the problem becomes "Where is the seriousness of purpose that is the other equally valid side of my dog stewarding value system?" Fun though it may be, caring for Kunio is not a game.

I guess I should be grateful I've got the main chapters in the bag. I never thought I'd be this close to finishing, but it's true what they say: Keep squeezing it out every day and it really does pile up.

Insight arrives via the dog of a stranger

The drummer in my band, the Cool Uncles, threw a party last spring and there was this guy there I hadn't met before, standing in the kitchen telling us about something that had happened when he was out birding at the Ballard Locks. "This hippie-ish couple show up with their dog," he said, "and proceed to remove the dog's

Preamble to "The Care and Feeding of Kunio While I'm in Mexico: Toward a Whole-Dog Approach" (Excerpt)

Hello! Come in! There's some green tea in the little Indian box thing by the stove—please help yourself. It's good stuff. The kind you can get at Safeway is fine in a pinch, but this is a batch I picked up special in Chinatown. At this little place you may not have heard of. Down a couple dark corners from the tourist-beaten path. Mr. Wui sees me coming and he practically has the stuff weighed out on the counter for me before I'm even in the door.

Practically. He does like to kid around by asking who I am, and if he's supposed to remember me or something. As if he didn't remember as well as I the hilarious exchange we shared no more than eight months ago, when I was ribbing him about how relations between Taiwan and China have *really* gone downhill lately.

After you've prepared your tea, please take a seat in the breakfast nook. Stop reading now and pick up again when you're settled in.

*

Comfy? If you kind of slouch down in your seat, you can see a little corner of Mount Baker under the eaves of those town homes over there. This is among the chief charms of the breakfast nook, along with the *Sibley Birds* calendar and little sparkly thing from Morocco dangling in the window. Go ahead and take a sip of tea and breathe consciously for a few minutes.

OK, this is where I have to confess something. I have an ulterior motive here. Partly, of course, I want you to relax simply because you're my friend, and I care about your mental health. But—and here we're starting to tickle the surface of my ulteriority—I have a few new ideas to present, and it's vitally important for you to be in as receptive a mood as possible.

Don't worry—of *course* we'll get to the mundane specifics of what to feed Kunio and how to retrieve his feces. Those are detailed in Chapter Four, laid out in chart form in Appendix Two, and summarized on a laminated card tucked in the back pouch of this binder. This card is for you to keep on your person at all times for the duration of your dog-sitting duties. Please also notice the emergency contact list on the back of the card.

But before we get into these specifics, I'd like to use the early chapters to discuss my overall philosophy of dog care. This discussion will culminate in ten principles that distill all previous material into a more easily memorized form.

But first—and I don't want you to be alarmed by this—I have to tell you that you're currently in violation of Principle the First: *Greet love with love.* It's very important that the first thing you do when you enter the house is to perform an expression of affection. This is especially true in my absence, when Kunio's liable to be in a fragile mental state and in need of a lot of assurance. For now you can utilize a simple calling out of his name in a warm voice followed by a series of head pats. Later we'll cover more complex greeting and rituals, including various pre- and post-walk absolutions.

For now, though, let's just rectify that little violation of yours. At this point, please put your tea down, exit the residence, close and lock the door, stand outside for a count of thirty, unlock the door, reenter the residence, and perform the basic greeting we just discussed.

We'll pick this up again when you get back.

leash and let him chase the birds I'm quietly watching." (I knew by "birds," he most likely meant goldeneyes, mergansers, and/or greater white-fronted geese, but let it pass for the moment.) "What is the deal," he asked, "with people and their dogs here?"

It's always awkward when someone expresses an opinion that everyone knows to be incorrect. Not that any opinion can be "incorrect," but there are opinions in need of correction. If you know what I mean. Look, everyone has a viewpoint, and that's valid. I'm a committed supporter of the validity of viewpoint-having. That's exactly why I try to be compassionate whenever it becomes necessary to administer a viewpoint correction. I urge you to do the same. Smother the discussion with a warm blanket of consensus. The best way to do this is through the use of a Git PaV, or Generalization in the Passive Voice. For example, "The key thing that should be understood here . . ." Other possibilities include "What hasn't been properly grasped is . . ." and "It's become clear that . . ." Then it's not your own opinion, it's just *the way it is*. And you're not attacking the individual person in front of you, you're talking about people in *general*. You, me, everyone—we *all* need to work on this thing here. As long as this big ol' goofy world has been spinning, people have learned at their own pace. You don't consider yourself better than anyone else just because you happen to be slightly more informed about an important issue than your neighbor. That's what these phrases convey. Remember, Don't git mad, Git PaV.

You can also try a "humorous" approach. A little bit of the funny goes a long way toward deflating dissent. You can say, "Whoa! Slow down there, Mr. Grumpy!" or "Oopsie boopsie, someone is being a wil' bit hasty!"

To that birder at the party I said, "Shazam, Shazbot, and Sha Na Na! It looks like it may be necessary to distribute a few fact-o-rinskis on this topic!" I then gently explained that the socio-ecosystem of a public beach is a delicate balance of humans and nature, rights and responsibilities. Nature has most of the rights, while we humans have most of the responsibilities. Dogs fit into this very subtly. A dog is a family member. A mini-human, if you will. That's one reason so many evening activities in Seattle are cut short—everyone has to rush home and attend to the bowel movements of these mini-humans. Stew in your microbrew alone at the bar as much as you want, I told him, but valuing the needs of an animal over interaction with other humans is a perfectly valid lifestyle choice. It's also why a dog at the beach holds the full rights of both nature and mini-humanity. This is comparable to how bicycles hold the rights of both car and pedestrian. (Need a refresher on this? Head on back to chapter 2!) To claim dogs aren't allowed to chase birds is like saying birds aren't allowed to eat worms. And about those birds in the birder's story. Just how natural were they anyway? Lounging about a park in the middle of the day? Something seemed kind of "off" about that. I found it hard to believe that they didn't have some foraging to do.

As the man at the party started to object, I deftly saved him from the embarrassment of being a conflict monger by offering him the balm of some much-needed empathy. "It *is* complicated, isn't it?" I said supportively. "Let's put a semicolon on this for now and come back to it some other time." He then suddenly announced he had to go let out his own dog. When it was pointed out that he had no dog, he said, "I meant my cat." I think the truth is he just wanted to be alone. After all, he had a lot to think about.

The only reason I even thought of that incident was because what I actually set out to do was share another story of insight delivered via the dog of a stranger. It plays out in an exchange with a man who's bothered, and may or may not be hot:

> *I was out with Hastings, my Labradoodle, at the park the other day when he spotted a frisky old French bulldog at the gate. They sniffed briefly, started playing together, and soon some action was going on, if you know what I mean. I thought little of it, but then a lady approached and asked point-blank if my dog was "intact." Confused but wanting to impress her, I said, "Um, sure, he likes to play around*

*a little." But I have no idea what she meant or why she was asking
me. Have you heard this expression? Do you think she was flirting?
She was quite a bit older than me. Was she tactless to ask?*

                    UP HALF THE NIGHT WONDERING

Dear Up Half the Night,

Do you have a problem with bulldogs generally? Or
French ones in particular? Maybe you have some unexamined hang-ups about your dog's sexuality?

Look at it this way: Opportunities for love are rare indeed.
That's something I found myself contemplating while cir-
cumambulating Green Lake on one of the perfect evenings
we've had recently. Watching the ghostly white peak of Mount
Rainier sliding along behind the trees, I reflected that . . .
Look, I'm not one to subject myself to a lot of self-criticism.
Inhale only positive energy, as my yoga teacher likes to say.
But if I were to make one self-observation, I might venture
to say that excessive taciturnity may be an impediment
to . . . What I'm trying to say is, I'm just not good at meeting
women.

I'm putting myself out there, OK? That was a moment
of real vulnerability I just offered you there and I hope
you'll respect my offering. A good faith effort in this direction would be admitting that you are indeed attracted to
the woman you mentioned, and that you know *exactly* what
she meant. Because that leads me to my main point, which
is that you can't ignore the issue of being intact vs. being
tactful.

You have the chance to be both. Your dog's impulse
toward the other dog is a wide boulevard, lined with spring
flowers, leading to the woman in the park. She's the one who
brought up your dog's equipment, so you can go with that
general topic without disrespecting her gender. A dome of
permission hangs over you, like Betty Friedan's fleshy face
smiling in the sky. If Betty Friedan's face could be somehow
inverted like the inside of a dome.

At any rate, progressive consciousness and animal instinct are moving in the same direction. Surrender to this harmonic convergence. Go back to the park with Hastings, and connect with that woman, as well as with your own slumbering state of intactness. When you get to know that woman better, you'll know for sure she's tactful. Because it'll be your tact she's full of.

A quick aside: What about cats?

We don't intend to exclude them here. I hope this exchange makes it clear in how much esteem I hold cats and their people:

The lady next door has about eighteen cats. Actually, about seventeen, since I backed over one the other day. Thing is, I don't think she's noticed. Do I have to tell her?

KITTY KILLER

Dear Killer,

I'm not going to pretend I'm a cat person, though of course cats are every bit as valid as dogs. Even if this is an animal known to sink its little stapler teeth into your wrist while it purrs with pleasure. Some of us need love that's a little less complicated. Indeed, the question must be asked, does a cat really die if no one hears its little kitty shriek of death? I'm not saying that the answer isn't yes, just that the question must be asked.

Another question: Where did you hide Mr. Tottingham? Dead cats are not appropriate for composting, unless you use the compost only for ornamentals. In which case you'll have particularly vivid marigolds next spring. The vividness of a recycled cat. If you present a freshly cut vase of these marigolds to your neighbor every week for two months, you can consider your debt paid. There's no need to offer any explanation. After all, unlike a cat, flowers don't stare at you with sleepy alien eyes, wishing very much that you were small enough to eat.

Speaking of death, what's the greenest way to dispose of a deceased doggie?

He hated fireworks. He knocked drinks over with his tail. He could bark at great length. His heart wished no other creature harm. He bit only one child. The whole thing was a big misunderstanding. Oh, sorry! You happened to catch me rehearsing a eulogy for my friend's dog. Timing is important in these things. You gotta figure out how to drop in jokes at the intervals that will most efficiently generate that laughter-through-the-tears effect and get the crowd on your side. I don't think I need to remind anyone how much he liked his soysauges! That's my first laugh line. It's scheduled to appear one minute and forty-eight seconds into the eulogy. I know, that seems too soon, right? That's what I thought, too, before I listened back to the run-through I taped on my webcam and realized just how long that is to go without a joke.

My friend hasn't actually asked me to deliver the eulogy, but I frankly find it hard to imagine who else he'd choose. Haven't I always been Coltrane's de facto godfather? His go-to human for tummy rubs and Sunday morning treats? Who better to commend his spirit to the great beyond with affection, gravitas, and those little touches of humor we were just discussing?

I guess I should also mention that the dog in question hasn't actually died. Yet! He's definitely not looking good though. I just get the sense that his earthly run is winding down. Admittedly, he appeared to have rallied a bit when I saw him yesterday sprinting around Green Lake. And of course that's a good thing. I'm still working the kinks out of my opening lines.

Barking dogs in passing cars

Well, it's time to wrap things up here in doggieland. I like to think that we've shared a carefully modulated mix of practical advice and higher truths. For further reference on this subject, please attend to barking dogs in passing cars. Absorb rather than resist the positive energy of this Doppler-warped barking. Try to see the dog in the car for what he is, a creature almost mad with the joy of the moment. So many interesting things are flashing by in such rapid succession that he's about to lose his little doggie mind. When he sees you, the most interesting thing in the last five seconds, it's all too much, and he just has to start barking. The barking may mean, "Hey! I'm going faster than you!" or, "Hey! Let's fight!" The specific meaning doesn't matter so much as the dog's overall point: Life is right now. Don't miss it.

That's how I hear it anyway. If to you it's just a nuisance, if you want to rush home to your reality television shows and remain unmoved by the simple animal wisdom shining in his brown eyes flashing by in that car window, that's the parade you choose to march in.

Your Kids

What do they want?

"More mouths, bigger foot" This phrase—meaning that every additional mouth results in a bigger human footprint on the earth—is not something I would mutter repeatedly under my breath while staring at my friends' children. That would be creepy. There are plenty of other ways to communicate this idea, like sing-songing it while pushing those kids on the swing.

Seriously though, I've already made it clear that I don't find anything weird about people who choose to have kids instead of dogs. Sure, sometimes those kids bother my Kunio when we go to the park. But I know the little ones are still learning how to coexist with dogs in public places. Respect a dog's space when he's nosing around the slide, OK, kiddos? In the interest of humans and animals sharing the park on an equal basis, don't make any sudden movements.

I'm a fan of kids and their wonderful creativity and so forth. But I'm also a fan of a more holistic awareness of the impact of human reproduction on the environment. So I thought I'd just jot down a few notes. *A Fan's Notes*, you might call them. Heh.

Apologies to all those not so burdened as I with an excessive love of books for whom that last reference might have gone whistling high overhead. I hope you could at least appreciate its after-plumes hovering in the sky. Because whenever I decide to proceed with an educated reference, I do try to make sure there is something in it for everyone, even if only the droll music of the words themselves. Indeed, those who get the reference but not the music are probably worse off than those who hear only the music. In other words, the smell of a banquet is more savory to the hungry man outside the castle walls than the taste of it is to those seated inside.

But there's no need to be a hungry man or woman outside *my* walls. Come in, sit down, and share a few of my ideas about your kids. I won't bite, and I promise not to use the whiteboard.

An idea came to me just now, as a matter of fact, a fun gift idea for the next baby shower you get invited to: a mini-landfill kit. The new parents can set it up in the backyard and fill it with poopy diapers and other trash produced by the baby, so the little one can see firsthand the bigger footprint she's helped create. It would also be terrific for the child, when she's old enough, to see the mountain of garbage that resulted from her birth.

I hope this idea shows you why I—a childless single man— presume to offer child-rearing advice. It's exactly *because* I have an outsider's perspective that I'll be able to knock you out of your paradigm a little bit here. Cushioning the blow with my own brand of wackiness, of course! Before we get there, though, let's start with the basics.

What do babies want?

I'm afraid that when I point out that they're increasing the burden on the earth in a way that threatens our very survival, people will think I'm anti-baby or something. Not true. I'm quite capable of dialoguing on human needs, and I include babies in the human category. I am, in short, a friend to babies.

But I can't help noticing that babies are terrible at pretty much everything they do. Including milk drinking, which should be a specialty of theirs. Every time they do it, they swallow a lot of air. Then they want to belch, but they can't. Because they're not good at that, either. Again, I'm not criticizing babies here, just making some observations.

One of the other things they want is to hold their oversized heads upright, which is always a struggle for them. I will say this, though, they do keep at it, a look of intense concentration on their wobbly little faces. When they take a break from that and lie on their backs, what they want is to control their hands, which tend to crash-land into their faces. If they somehow manage to get hold of something, like their own heads, they're amazed and want to know what it is. Some of them want that noise to stop. Or that dog over there to go away and/or to come closer so they can poke its eyeballs.

Have you noticed that babies also tend to stare a lot? As they're carried about in those little backpacks they think nothing of gazing at you for minutes on end. They do this without a word of reprimand from anyone. I've tried to step in occasionally to fill the education gap, keeping my tone as friendly as possible. "Hey," I'll reason with them quietly when their parents aren't looking, "Did you know most people think staring is kind of rude? We're all just people here, my friend." Unfortunately, their lack of skills also extends to basic language comprehension.

I'm guessing they stare because they're simply puzzled. They're easily puzzled. And easily amused by actions such as yawning or taking out your car keys. There's really no telling with babies. Like I said, I'm not making judgments. Babies are doing the best they can. It's just that their best happens to be not so hot.

Toilet training

Babies do eventually grow and become a bit more recognizably human. As they do, they must be taught to be polite. And an important part of being polite is not pooping in your pants. While I'm no expert on child-rearing, I do know that shame is bad, and would like to outline a shame-free approach to the potty issue that you may find helpful.

After all, when he has an "accident," your child is just doing what comes naturally—really no worse than me slipping off my sports sandals and giving myself a little foot massage, no matter where I happen to be. A coffee shop, a restaurant, my doctor's waiting room—most any place is good for a vigorous self-rubbing. If other people have a problem with my level of bodily comfort, that's their pie to slice.

You, too, need to readjust the way you see your child's bodily functions. Focus on the positive and gently redirect his impulses. Suggest that, as wonderfully luxurious as it may be to take a crap in your pants, sitting on the toilet can be even better. Tell him not to force the rhythm, to let it come to him. The right reading material is essential—stay away from the *Nation*, or anything else that may get him riled up about the state of the world. I suggest *100 Poems from the Japanese*. While other bells that will toll in his future may be less pleasant (adolescence, death), there's no reason why this particular call of nature can't be an occasion for contemplative repose.

Moms! Moms! Moms!

Sorry, I didn't mean to shout the word "moms" three times. It does seem like a good way to mark the start of the section though. Sort of a little fanfare to make it clear that I'm not anti-mom any more than I'm anti-baby.

I was thinking of this the other day when I saw a young mom whose galoshes brought a real trumpet blast of good cheer to my day. They were green with yellow polka dots. She had tucked her jeans into them and was marching through the rain with an armful of toddler. Holy Osh Galosh B'Gosh, was she ever cute as a button! I mean that in a respectful, non-objectifying way. My mom never wore colorful galoshes. I think adults back then were more serious. Young moms today seem like they're having so much fun. Not that Mom didn't have fun, but it was just different back then.

I admire the style of the current crop of moms. Just the other day I found myself at a dinner party, sipping Pinot and admiring the tasteful nude photograph of my hostess framed next to the iPod cradle, standing serenely in profile in front of a black background, her right hand laid over her left breast and her left hand cupped over the soft swell of her pregnant belly. I appreciated the photograph's qualities at some length. I like to think I've got a good eye for artistically presented mom-bits.

That's all by way of introducing you to some pretty special moms who've come at various times to "kick it" with me in my column. I like to think of the column as a place where women, especially mom women, can talk about absolutely anything. I think one reason they trust me is that I don't pretend to have The Answer, which is probably a refreshing change from the usual pushy males in their lives. Also, I have realistic expectations about what an advice column can actually accomplish. If sparks from the high-voltage tension between what I say and what I leave unsaid continue to flicker in their mind, illuminating unexpected moments of their lives for years to come, I'll consider that to be success.

With a little bow then, I now present to you a bouquet of voices plucked from the mom community. Bonus points if you spot the motif running through my answers. Think of it as a scavenger hunt. Remember, Rule One is Rule Fun!

I breastfed my five-month-old daughter during the first three months, but I've been doing a mix of breast- and bottle-feeding since I went back to work. So there I was, sitting with a group of Seattle moms at the park, when I pulled out her bottle, and a hush fell over the group. Then this mom with a preschooler hanging on her nipple asked if I was worried that my daughter and I would fail to bond properly. How do I tell this self-appointed band of breast vigilantes that my kid and I are bonded just fine?

ANNOYED MOM

Dear Annoyed Mom,

I'm glad you asked. I'm actually rather qualified to answer, because I'm so comfortable discussing women's bodies. In particular, their breasts. Their breasts and their nipples. I can say the word "nipple" out loud in public without a problem. Nipple, nipple, nipple! See? No big thing. I'm very informed about women's health issues and can discuss them in a progressive way, without discomfort. You could even call me Dr. Nipple. Hahahaha! I mean, you know, if you wanted to. Sorry, I didn't mean anything by that.

What was your question again? Oh yes. Breast-feeding. Feeding from your breasts, using your nipples. A natural, natural question. So you are breast-feeding and want some advice about your breasts? And your nipples? Like I said, I'm glad you asked.

First of all, it's very natural for new mothers to feel over-whelmed. Heck, even I get a bit overwhelmed sometimes—even if I don't have breasts! Or nipples. Wait. I do. Not breasts, but nipples. Hahaha! Whee! OK, try to relax. You're in good hands here. I mean, haha, so to speak.

I bet if you asked some of those other mothers, they could give you some pointers about breasts. As I understand it, breast-feeding is always best and there is a single correct way of parenting. I'll bet there are some brochures they could give you about this. And anything else you wanted to know about breasts and nipples.

But I should mention in parting that your notion of an actual band of breast vigilantes is quite fanciful, and may reveal that your postpartum condition has rendered you slightly paranoid. Again, this is a natural reaction for new mothers, and not something over which you should beat up those nipples of yours. ☺

I was leaving the Bakery a while back with a baby and a four-year-old in tow when a man followed me out the door to point out, accusingly, that we were expected to bus our own tables. I had not done so but was taken aback by his pursuit. While I admit I transgressed, is it reasonable to police the busing behaviors of others?

BUSTED

Dear Busted,

Taken aback by a pursuit? Sounds like we have some serious directional dysfunction here. Energy is being cast forward and pulled back in highly contradictory ways!

Hey, don't look so tense! I know that was gibberish. I

was just messing with you a little there to loosen you up.
When we're touchy and defensive, we're likely to be less
open-minded about learning from our mistakes, wouldn't
you agree? So, relax—I'm not conducting a police interroga-
tion here!

Keeping that in mind, let's go through the timeline one
more time. I assume there was some kind of emergency.
Maybe one of your children, or both of them, were bleeding
from the neck? In such a situation, yes, of course, it might
well be understandable that you wouldn't do a full clearing
of your table (though you could have perhaps at least thrown
away your trash).

Or did you mention your children for some other reason? I'll give you the benefit of the doubt and assume that
you didn't expect that the cafe, or society as a whole, would
accord you some sort of special treatment because you
reproduced.

Let's back up a moment and imagine this situation
from the man's perspective. He's quietly going about his
business—drinking his coffee, reading his paper, and moni-
toring you and your kids. Sure, he thinks, that woman
may have children, but that doesn't necessarily mean she's
insensitive about the larger footprint she therefore makes
on the earth. I'm sure she will, if anything, be even more
diligent about her responsibilities. She certainly wouldn't
expect minimum-wage workers to clean up after her. Or so
he thinks.

And then he sees you get up and leave trash strewn all over
the table, a mound of diapers on the floor, and perhaps a trail
of blood-soaked rags from your children's neck wounds. As
if the words "please bus your own table" in sun-faded marker
were not affixed with four yellowing pieces of cellophane tape
above the cream station. The man could have simply shaken
his head sadly and gone back to his soy latte. But no, he seized
the teaching moment and charged aggressively across the
wide meadow that separates stranger from stranger. I suggest
you meet him halfway, at the Learnin' Tree.

My child is gifted. Her friends are not. How can I avoid making their parents self-conscious about this difference?

ZOE'S MOM

Dear Zoe's Mom,

One word: Disney. From their latest assembly-line tween sitcom to their juggernaut of sterile pop music, Disney is the biggest thing among non-gifted families right now. Bone up on their entertainment products so you can respectfully relate to these regular folks on their own terms. Instead of waiting for them to awkwardly happen upon your higher cultural terrain of drama, jazz history, and autobiographical studies, charge down into their crass valley. The next time you're chatting on the sidelines of a soccer game, ask them with a laugh if they, too, are being dragged to the latest release from the studio. And if they are headed to the nearest big-box chain store to pick up the new DVD. Consult advertisements for the relevant release dates, which form a kind of holy calendar to these families. Even if they see through your efforts to the inner giftedness of your family, they'll certainly appreciate your effort to reach down to them.

The following question appeared on the application to a preschool for my son: "What will you bring to our community?" Excuse me? Is it a child-care service or a freakin' cult? Maybe I'm overreacting, but I don't know whether to be more offended by the absurdly misplaced elitism or the touchy-feely disguise it's wearing.

MIFFED MOM

Dear Mom,

Instead of getting bogged down in second-guessing the preschool's motivations, why not focus on the many assets that I'm sure you *can* bring to the community if you try? Everyone has something special to offer. Can you bake bread? Can you sing? Sure you can. Everyone can sing! Or maybe you're that really good knot undoer everyone brings their extra-troublesome knots to. Hey! Do you have a special silly dance you do when no one else is around? I bet you do. Why not come out of that shell of yours and share your silly dance with the world? With all the craziness these days, well, we all sure could use a smile about now.

Not to belittle kids with allergies, because I know allergies are real and can be deadly. But there do seem to be an awful LOT of allergic kids around these days. It seems like everyone and their kids are now allergic to something or other. It's common for a fellow parent to tell me that their child needs a gluten-, lactose-, and processed-sugar-free diet or she will get dry skin and/or become psychotic. What are people doing to their kids?

DON'T FEAR THE SANDWICH

Dear Sandwich,

When regular people are interviewed on television because they've witnessed some horrible accident, they use the word "basically" a lot. "The whole thing basically went up in flames," they say, "and we all basically ran away." Is there anything wrong with that? Of course not. It's perfectly understandable if these regular ol' hardworkin' folks don't happen to be as articulate as someone who, for example, has a master's degree. To each her or his own. And in the same way, there's nothing wrong with you, Sandwich, if you don't happen to be sensitive enough for food allergies.

See, sensitive people know there's a lot wrong with the world. Chemicals and other evils fairly shimmer in the air before their eyes. Their bodies are finely tuned to the subtle evil lurking even in seemingly safe substances such as wheat. (And if you listen closely, even the sound of the word "wheat" is sort of sinister, like it could be the past tense of "we." Do you know from your own direct experience that wheat does not in fact herald a cold new post-we realm of solitary "mes" and "yous"? If not, could it be that you shouldn't ridicule the idea?)

Children of sensitive people, especially if these sensitive people have a lot of money, are introduced to this evil, wheaty shimmer through a carefully blended private-school curriculum of theater, labor history, and autobiographical studies. Through years of careful effort, the sensitivity of these people and their kids may be honed to such a hyper-fine perfection of intolerance that it gives off a kind of ambient glow. You may find it a little unsettling to pass through this soft, golden light, Sandwich, and you interpret this unsettling feeling as irritation. But you might consider making yourself a list of more constructive attitudes, including quiet awe, humble gratitude, and nonchalant jocularity.

How can I get my daughter to practice piano?
                                        UNTICKLED IVORY

Dear Ivory,

Sure do love that Norah Jones. Diana Krall, too, and a number of other talented piano ladies who are bringing back old-fashioned class and musicianship. When I saw Norah at Key Arena, the crowd was almost entirely made up of white males my age. We were all avoiding eye contact with each other for some reason. Anyway, you should tell your daughter that practice, practice, practice is the only way to attract an audience like us.

Did you catch the motif in my answers? If you said "a completed circuit," hooray for you! It's what I like to imagine as a mischievous little snake slithering between *intentional being* and *being intentional*. Slither slither here, slither slither there, and zap! Circuit completed.

Now let's hear from a dad

Not me. I'm not a dad. I've got an idea for a dad book though. It would be called *The Poor Farmer and the Angry Goddess: Using Myth to Explain Your Divorce to Your Kids*. It would be an ego-free production. The insights in it would not be from me, per se. I would be merely a conduit of lore. A lore conduit. Because lore has been lost. If I could play even a small part in reconnecting dads and lore, that would be the only thanks I'd need.

My techniques are simple, but they can even be applied to the sticky subject of teen sexuality. For example, a friend recently told me that he'd found evidence his teenage son had been looking at Internet porn. "Asian bondage sluts," that kind of thing. I urged him first of all not to panic. The vigorously wagging tail of a young man's sexuality may be unnerving, but there's nothing wrong with appreciating a woman's beauty. It's just that this must be done in a respectful, holistic fashion.

How to get this across to a teenage mind? Well, a truly advanced being will find that the most arousing sight in the world is a waterfall. Contemplate it for a moment: a streaming mass of mountain rain, drawn with irresistible force toward a crashing, foamy reunion with the earth. My point is that sexuality is best conceived as a disembodied force of the universe. Especially if you happen to hit a five-year dry spell or two.

So if you find yourself in my friend's position, here's what you should do: Redirect your son's enthusiasm toward this higher spiritual element. Take him to a Japanese flower-arrangement demonstration, and let him observe a demure middle-aged lady erecting branches and lilies in an asymmetrical orange vase. Murmur softly to him, "Son, if you think about it, the flower sensei is really the greatest Asian slut of them all. For she so freely gives the world access to the soft, delicate beauty she has inside." The thoughtful, far-off look you see in his eyes will be the evidence of your fatherly success in taking control of his sexual imagination.

*

But sometimes it's a father's own wandering imagination that must be redirected:

> *I saw this place the other day called Playmatters, which billed itself as "a place for kids to play and parents to network." Is this secretly a place to hook up with MILFs on the make? If so, the fifteen bucks a visit seems like a bargain. Otherwise, I don't see paying for the privilege of sitting in a room with my kid for an hour, even if it does have Wi-Fi and wooden toys from Sweden.*
>
> ME NO PAY NO PLAY DOUGH

Dear Me No Pay No,

When I was on my retreat at the Ananda Meditation Retreat Center last year, we had a question-and-answer session with the center's Head Seeker. He offered the same response to every question: "Look inward." And those are the words I was at first tempted to offer you, Me No Pay No. Then I looked in the mirror and laughed (a healthy exercise I would recommend for everyone!). For who am I to think I've attained the status of Head Seeker, or even Regular Ol' Seeker?

So let me instead be a little more specific: Have you heard of pre-mail? That's when you write an e-mail before the issue it addresses has become an issue. A technologically forward community must from time to time coin such terms. Like when we noticed back in the nineties that Starbucks was a third place outside of work and home, and so started talking about "the third place." Just so, Playmatters has adopted the use of "network" as a verb to describe what happens there. Calling it "a place for parents to meet" would not speak to the delicate sensitivity to sociological truths nurtured by a certain level of education, nor to the material benefits of those truths. Maybe all this gives you a feeling of exclusion. And feelings are a great place to start! But I'm sure those other parents would be just as happy to "network" with you even if you're a public school custodian or a newspaper delivery driver.

A word about saving the placenta

Some parents are bound to absorb all this information more easily than others. Find your own position on the some/others spectrum by answering the following question: Are you horrified by the practice of keeping the placenta in the freezer after a baby is born? If yes, then you probably want to reinvest in your awareness level by rereading this chapter in a week or so. You may find that a gem can sparkle from more than one angle. In the meantime, I don't want to just leave you alone with the placenta, so let me offer some points for contemplation.

Instead of feeling horror, perhaps you should feel respect. Because I'm pretty sure that freezing a placenta is some kind of Native American tradition or something. That you feel disgusted could mean you've discovered a crucial contradiction in your thinking. After all, there are two or more things that emerge in the birth process. Why should we value one over the other? Native Americans and other people with lore understood this. It is only our *Homo sapiens*–centric viewpoint that makes us cherish the infant and discard the afterbirth, a term with prejudice built into it. After all, we don't call the baby "prebirth."

Crazy? Maybe. Think of this, though: If you cut your head from your body, into which part would your "I" go? Would you say "me and my body" or "me and my head"? It's like that horror/respect conundrum. I'm not trying to force you to believe anything in particular, I'm just trying to make you think. The last time I checked, that was still in the Constitution.

And finally, the voice of a child

We can't possibly close on this topic without touching on the other side of the kids equation: the kids! Stepping up to the mike now is a little girl with a common complaint:

My dad is a piece of shit.

                                              AN 8-YEAR-OLD

Dear 8-Year-Old,
    My first instinct is to argue along these lines: The state of being you characterize as "a piece of shit" may be only a brief stop on a journey toward new spring growth. You seem to be a bright young person, so perhaps you've followed my past discussions of the golden value feces has in Gaia's manure-for-daisies-based economy that we're all part of in some way. Therefore, my argument would go, your piece-of-shit dad may have more to offer than you think.
    But instead, I would like to tell you about a friend of mine and his daughter. I'm guessing you and your dad may be like these two. If so, your dad is sometimes unable to cope with the speed and energy of your mind, a magically sensitive instrument sorting through the rich experience of being alive, from Pokémon and best friends to astronomy and cursive Ls. His mind is a bit sluggish in comparison. This difference in speed may sometimes make him irritable, especially when he's out of vodka. But your burgeoning powers light him up with an incandescent joy, even when you're reading the phone book instead of getting dressed for school, or testing the water resistance of his iPod. When you beat him at chess for the first time the other day, it was a defeat sweeter than a thousand victories. And that's no shit.

Relationships

Flexibility and resourcefulness

We're so resistant to stillness in our society. I was thinking about this when I went to a party the other day. Owing to my reflective mood at the time, I didn't care to join the dancing at this party, but thought the admirably festive spirit of the dancers shouldn't pass without some expression of my approval. So I went to the center of the dance floor and struck a yoga pose of my own invention, the Half-Napping House Cat. It's a loungey kinda pose, part watchful and part playful. In other words, just perfect for the occasion. I sort of hung there for a couple songs in my pose, which involves a lolling head and a sleepy cat's frozen grin. I was perfectly still and perfectly content. Later I heard that some people at the party were apparently offended by my display. Imagine! Being offended by stillness!

The point is, I'm single. So I might not be the world's biggest authority on relationships. All I'm offering here are a few observations. Take 'em or leave 'em. Or do something else with 'em entirely, like leaving 'em out in the sun until they get all dry and crinkly. I don't take it personally when people are, for whatever reason, unable to open their spirit to one of my observations and free themselves from the destructive power of their own assumptions.

Like women who unquestioningly take up the trappings that society imposes on their gender. Red lipstick, high heels, tight skirts, and silky blouses. Creams to make their skin soft and fragrant. And whatever product that makes their floral-scented hair catch the light just so. All of which I observe on the bus, in coffee shops, and waiting in line at the bank.

You'll remember though that we talked in the last chapter about how there's nothing wrong with admiring a woman in a respectful way. There are a number of, well, total babes in my reading group. But they would never wear low-slung jeans or tops that would reveal the milky-smooth skin of their midriffs. Not that I actually notice *what* they wear—their dog-hair-covered Gore-Tex jackets, their tiny spectacles and limp ponytails. I don't notice any of that. They can see by the way I smile at them that I'm not noticing what they wear. And that I appreciate their indifference to superficial things. I try not to wave my sensitivity in their faces though.

What I'm trying to get at here is that there are often women involved in relationships, so it only seems fair that I should lay out my cards on the topic. Now, I'm not going to be so patriarchal as to claim I've solved Freud's misogynistic "puzzle" as to what women want, but perhaps it won't cause offense if I start off by telling you about something that happened to me the other day at work.

Female Co-worker A asked me what I thought about Female Co-worker B. When I said I had no particular opinion, she pressed the issue. Didn't I think that Female Co-worker B was "kind of weird"? After further hints and wordless grimaces, I finally ascertained that Co-worker A thought Co-worker B was funny-looking and a slut, and was hoping I would join her in this opinion.

I mention this because I'm pretty sure there's a clue here. Not sure what it is though. A friend once told me that sometimes women just want you to be their ally, and that this can entail simply listening sympathetically, even if you can't understand everything they say. I didn't want to embarrass him by pointing out that he was making a paternalistic generalization. Maybe I'll slip him an anonymous note.

✻

Even if you do make an effort to bridge that communication gap, you may hit a dry period with the opposite sex. A period that may last as long as, for example, five years, eight months, three weeks, and one day. During such a period, you may become vulnerable to feelings of resentment. Especially if you happen to see women who are attracted in an inappropriate way to men who aren't you.

Like maybe there's a block party in your neighborhood, the firefighters from the neighborhood station show up with huge platters of barbecued ribs, and you witness some of your female neighbors behaving in an overly solicitous manner toward these firefighters. To be taken in by their broad shoulders, dazzling smiles, and kindness to children—well, it's frankly a little shocking that women would be willing to so casually betray their long struggle for equality. Did the women in this purely hypothetical example even bother to check these firefighters' voting records before talking to them? Were the ribs even organic?

The very sight of some couples can strain the imagination to the breaking point. But remember that the imagination can be a dangerous thing. I saw this particular couple once, and while I don't exactly regret what happened—I don't believe in regret—it turned out that the woman was not in fact blinking out the Morse code for "Please help. I'm being held against my will." I suggest you, too, beware of dark imaginings. Focus instead on your own love life. I may be in a bit of a slump in that department myself, but that doesn't mean I don't live in hope. How else is there to live? I even had a date recently.

Well, it looks like the wine is all gone. I've had a great time, and I think we *both* learned a lot. We'll have to do this again sometime. Whoa, what was that? Were you just doing The Reach? Where you start reaching for the check, but in a way that betrays hope that someone will stop you? Why would I stop you? I think I've made it clear that I respect women too much for that. Besides, both of us just ate a nearly equal dollar amount of food. Actually, and not that I was adding it up or anything, you did have the clams and pasta dish, which I am pretty sure was around $21, and I had the mushroom ravioli, which was only $18. It was quite filling for the price, especially with all that bread they kept bringing. I don't recall who had more bread, though I definitely didn't have more than four pieces total, and there were about seven pieces in each basket. It doesn't matter anyway because the bread's free. Then there was the wine, which you picked out. I probably wouldn't have paid $27 for any Oregon pinot, much less that one. Despite all the hype, it's way too rainy there to produce grapes with any real character. So, to summarize my position, I don't see why I should pay the entire bill.

You are perhaps hoping I will rise, like an eagle from a dark valley, toward a perspective that encompasses not only myself but at least one other human being. OK, fair enough. But there's a larger point here, which is I don't *blame* you for any limitations in your way of seeing things. We're all doing the best we can.

To prove there are no hard feelings, I'll offer the following advice in exchange for you paying your part of the bill. The Reach must be executed with a swift, kung-fu-ian sincerity. Otherwise, you'll fumble all the way to actually paying, and feel silly besides. I've had quite a bit of luck with my own warriorlike commitment to The Reach.

The look on your face suggests that I'm not going to be particularly lucky tonight however.

Relationship Issuefest

There's no time to lollygag around the table anyway. Let's make tracks out of that little introductory ramble and get to the heart of this chapter. The most important part of any relationship is identifying, and working on, "issues." Here are some that have come up for my readers:

Self-conscious about my new boyfriend's thinning hair, I blurted out to my friends that he has cancer. Is it OK to ask him to play along?
                                        GIRLFRIEND WITH A BALDY

Dear Girlfriend,
    A crackling current runs through a new relationship, generated by the unspoken struggle for dominance. Who'll

be on top and who'll live in fear of being dumped? That's how I remember it, anyway, though it's been a while. That kind of grappling doesn't generally work out for me somehow. I'm better at scaling a hill in a national park than winning a heart in a natural chest. But let's reach back through all the preceding hill-grappling to reconnect with the electricity in the first sentence. Ride this playful, dangerous energy toward a thrillingly unpredictable ending. Look him in the eyes and ask: "What can I do for you in exchange for your feigning cancer tonight?"

I'm Japanese, and I don't know how to tell my American girlfriend that instead of "Power and Wisdom," her kanji tattoo actually says, "Afternoon Cow."

A FELLOW PACIFIC RIMMER

Dear Rimmer,

I have some stuff I've been saving up for just the right person, and I think you might be that person. Hang on a sec, let me get out my Moleskine. "Have an honest introspective." "Are you willing to make this idea authentic?" "Have the courage to interrogate reality." And this last one is really the kicker for your case, Rimmer: "The conversation IS the relationship." Got it? If none of that does it for you, get your own tattoo on some part of your body she's sure not to miss, one that says, "I love me some cow," and then give her a kanji dictionary as a gift to mark the end of Daylight Savings Time.

My girlfriend's great, but there's one problem: her cell phone ring. It's that C+C Music Factory song. Grounds for separation?

EVERYBODY DON'T DANCE NOW

Dear Everybody Don't,

BUMP. BUMP. Da-da-BUMP. BUMP. Da-da . . . Then the background rhythm thing comes in—shikashikashika shikashikashikashika—with the cowbell going, and you're a stronger man than I if you can keep still at that point. You ever have one of those days when you have a hard time getting going? Maybe you're thinking of friends who have passed on, or things that have never happened for you like you once thought they would. And then that song comes on, maybe in a commercial or something? I can still picture the African-American bodybuilder who sang it. Anyway, when you hear that song or even just think of it, don't you feel a little better right away? I know I do.

That reminds me of the other day when I took a little candy cane from the lobby of a bank. I don't usually eat mainstream sweets. I prefer traditional confectionary over the products of Big Cand. Fine, flaky confectionary. I only took the candy cane because it was butterscotch flavored, and I was expecting something like the butterscotch candy I remembered from my youth. The first time I had one was when Widow Johnson came out with a basket of them for us kids, who until that moment were sure she was a witch. But the butterscotch component of the candy cane from the bank was just a thin strip corkscrewed through the main candy cane material. The taste was but a sad echo of the rich flavor of so many summers ago.

I bring this up only because that's just what *isn't* the case with this song. It still works at full strength all these years later. And how many things can you—shikashikashikashik ashikashikashika!—say that about?

I hope you can take it like you dish it out because I've got a "gentle reminder" for you. What you referred to in your last response as a cowbell in "Gonna Make You Sweat (Everybody Dance Now)" is in fact an agogo bell. If only I had your powers of expression, I could more properly formulate my question, but alas, this is the best I can do: Into what hole will you now slink?

DRUMMER MAN

Dear Drummer Man,

Wow, your energy, it's fantastic! Don't look now, but I think all four elements on your chakric slot machine have come up fire. A fierce quadruple blaze! I thank you indeed for that refreshing blast. You must feel better than Chuck Mangione right about now.

Thanks also for the intriguing point you raise about agogo bells. I love it when a regular person such as yourself takes an interest in music. Don't you agree that the arts are just so important? I am glad that, to go along with the runaway train of your honesty, you have at least a glimmer of these larger issues as well. After all, great minds discuss ideas, mediocre minds discuss events, and poor minds discuss people. Don't you agree?

But even though it hardly warrants mentioning, so long as we're on this more trivial ground, let's just take a quick look at the Wikipedia entry for agogo bells. "They are," it says, "a kind of cowbell." Well! Whaddya know? Kinda funny how these things turn out, huh? Fate is indeed a mischievously spinning wheel, one moment lifting us up to the sky, the next moment depositing us in a deep hole, much like the one you just suggested for me. What can you do but laugh at the tricks she plays? Maybe another day and another turn of the wheel will cause our positions to be switched, with you up high and me down low. Of course, you know, maybe not.

As a twenty-two-year-old bisexual foreign girl I have to agree that American girls are in general very hot. But the other day a not-so-graceful girl came to me clearly trying to make more than

friends, and I didn't feel flattered at all. Actually I felt quite the
opposite of it. Am I becoming the kind of person who girls used to
name "jerk"? Should I feel bad about the negative feeling for this
girl?

A SENORITA ABROAD

Dear Senorita,

Foreign? And bisexual, too—extra credit! Are you also
in a wheelchair? Sorry, maybe I shouldn't have asked that.
I'm really not one of those Ugly Americans who doesn't even
try to pronounce foreign words correctly. When a barista
asks me, "What kind of cra-SANT do you want?" I reply with
a careful lingering over the correct pronunciation. "Hmm,"
I say, "I could have the plain cwa-SOHW, but, on the other
hand, the almond cwa-SOHW also looks rather delicious."
Commit random acts of education, that's my motto. Oh, and
this is just a general FYI, a Japanese bed isn't a FOO-tahn,
it's a foo-tone. Exercise restraint in the aspiration of the f,
and place no stress on either syllable. Let's all say it together
ten times: foo-tone, foo-tone, foo-tone, foo-tone, foo-tone,
foo-tone, foo-tone, foo-tone, foo-tone, foo-tone. It's actually
kind of soothing.

Anyway, can you tell me a little bit more about you and
the American girls that you find "hot"? As an advice columnist, I think it would be useful to know how you meet these
girls and what exactly you do with them. How does it work?
Of course, I know how it works. I'm a man of the world and
totally at ease here, but I just mean, in your particular case,
what's it like with the wheelchair and everything? Please
get back to me with these details and I will do my best to
help you.

When your relationship causes problems for your other relationships

~~~

There is a whole species of other problems that can arise between your partner and the other people in your life. There's no time to go into all of them, but I would like to present a little trick that could be of use to you with regard to these problems. It comes in response to a woman who turned up in my inbox all tied up in knots of her own devising:

I got this voice mail from my mom. Only she thought she'd called my sister. Her message was about me, and what a huge mistake it is for me to move in with my boyfriend. I was so mad, I called my sister and, pretending I thought I'd called my mom, left a message telling Mom she should stop telling everyone in town that my sister sleeps around. I've basically destroyed my family.

CHINESE-AMERICAN WHISPERER

Dear Whisperer,

Holy Shiva! That's one pretzel you won't be able to unbake easily! But I think one last swig from the Pandora's Merlot you've uncorked might do the trick. Call your mom and pretend you're your sister and that you mistakenly think you've called you. As your sister, say that you're worried your mom thinks you (that is to say, your sister) believe she (Mom) really said those horrible things about her (your sister). Say you forgive your sister (yourself) for manufacturing the whole thing, and that it's understandable since she (you) is (are) so emotional about her (your) burgeoning adult independence, which she (you) is (are) demonstrating with this impending move. Finally, say that since you (all of you) will always need and love each other no matter who moves in with whom, none of this nonsense really matters.

Click! That, Whisperer, is a little trick I like to call passive affection.

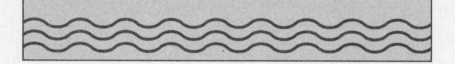

I'm in a relationship with this great woman, but she's got this one weird problem and it's starting to freak me out. Once a month, her vagina starts to bleed. Should I try to be supportive, or stop trying to accept something that makes me so uncomfortable and move on?

WILTING WALTER

Dear Walter,

Have you ever noticed that public bus drivers come in two basic varieties, grumpy and cheerful? My theory is that, washed in a river of unwashed humanity, they're forced to do one of two things: roll with it or fight it. Those who roll with it seem to acquire a rosy glow of contentment. They smile while strangers bark "back door!" at them. They can gracefully wrestle a sixty-foot articulated monster around a narrow corner while bantering with an old lady. The other ones though, the ones who fight it? They curtly dismiss lost tourists. They're disgusted when you don't know the fares went up last week. They do not offer a welcoming spirit when you enter their space. See, Wilting, it's just as Tom Robbins once observed, there are only two mantras: Yum and Yuck. I met Tom at a party once. I'm not claiming any special relationship or anything, but he did laugh at my Bruce Lee joke.

What does this have to do with your problem? Go to a Chinese restaurant to find out. The Jade Pagoda, where Bruce Lee used to wash dishes, isn't around anymore. Some other Chinese restaurant will do. Go and order a dish you've never had before. I'm guessing you'll discover that a thing that initially makes you uncomfortable can turn out to be delicious. Or it could be that you just don't like Chinese food. Maybe you like Greek food. And that's OK! But you should let Chinese food know right away.

I recently got a number of precancerous lesions removed from my skin. When I went home and my wife saw how many little bandages I had on my face and arms, she said, "Whoa, someone went hog wild!" as if I'd had them all removed for fun. What the heck?
                                                  GOTHIC HOBO JOE

Dear Gothic Hobo Joe,

Pardon me for asking this, but this information is crucial to my answer: Are you sort of a pain in the ass to her sometimes? As best I've been able to observe, any marriage is full of subtextual attacks and counterattacks that occur in a pattern comprehensible only to the couple themselves. Outsiders will have no idea what invisibly simmering feud compels one member of a couple at a dinner party to sneer to the other, "That couldn't have been the Spain trip, honey. Tyler hadn't even started kindergarten then." Having not yet found the person who completes me, I sometimes fantasize about my friends' wives. But not in the way you think. I imagine what it would be like to be emotionally eviscerated in public by these women. At those moments, the gray skies of my singlehood seem suddenly clearer.

But at other times, such as when I'm recumbently cycling home alone after those dinner parties, I imagine how I might respond differently if I were in the husband's place. I like to think I'd good-naturedly admire the skill of my wife's attack and offer with mock solemnity my flag of surrender as if it were the gift of a new courtship. I don't claim, Gothic Hobo Joe, that your wife deserves such a lavish gift. But perhaps you could instead think of it as a gift to your marriage itself.

My parents fight a lot. Are they going to get divorced?
                                        SAD SECOND-GRADER

Dear Second-Grader,
    You know what oil is? Dinosaur bones! Pretty neat, huh? But oil doesn't last forever. Despite this fact, our energy paradigm remains a self-destructively petroleum-centric one. Your parents' relationship is analogous to oil usage in that it seemed like a good idea at one point but now faces an uncertain future. Now, have you heard about wind power? That's when they make electricity with these cool windmill things in a big green field. Smart people call that a "renewable energy source." That means it has no end. Which is just like the love your parents have for you, no matter how much they act like big dummy heads to each other. So remember that wind lasts forever, and hang in there, OK, kiddo?

Singlehood

Which reminds us that sometimes the hardest part of a relationship is not having one. Especially on Valentine's Day. The situation has improved among kids. Just as a poison sac might be extracted from a pet cobra, so has any expression of affection been safely removed from Valentine's Day for children. It used to be that schoolkids would get cards from other kids who liked them, but the rule now is that if you bring cards, you have to bring them for everyone. No one gets hurt feelings, because the cards mean nothing.

Jottings from my Moleskine

Why doubt things unseen? You can't see love. You can't see your skeleton, but try standing up without it. Try doing a silly little dance without it. Actually that *would* be a silly dance!

But unfortunately, all kids will awake one harsh morning to the unsupervised horror of Valentine's Day in the grown-up world. While we wait for the necessary reforms to be enacted, I recommend that all victims of this holiday greet Valentine's Day with a spirit of defiance. Don't shrink from the red glow of its evil heart. No one needs you? So what! You need no one! Parade your goofy grin about town like a balloon on a string. Cultivate the swagger of a one-person submarine pilot. Now off to your quarters to down a stiff one while watching a Netflix DVD in your smoking jacket and feathered hat. Feel free to swap in whatever scenario makes you feel the most dashing and comfortable. Because good things happen when you loosen up a little.

One particularly rough Valentine's Day I'd actually put on *three* hats and was holding my head at an angle to keep the topmost hat from falling off. When it finally did fall off, there nestled inside of it were my glasses, which I'd been looking for all day. A Valentine's Day gift from my head to me. Even if you're not quite as tuned in as me to the possibilities tucked magically inside the mechanics of everyday life, I just bet this year's V-Day will bring you your own string of whimsical little victories.

✳

You will have to come out of that cozy bunker at some point though. Here are some of the dilemmas my single readers have shared with me. We'll start with a man who's disturbed by something his friend is getting and he is not:

My friend and I were both single for a long time, then he got a girlfriend. I'm happy for him, really. But now he makes these "sly" references to his love life pretty much nonstop. Like if we're eating something, he'll say, "This is good. Not as tasty as Carol though!" and point his waggling tongue at the ceiling. Or when he's leaving my house he'll say, "Well, I got something IMPORTANT to do," and then start pumping his fists at his hips and making a pop-pop-pop sound with his lips. Ugh!

GROSSED OUT GUS

Dear Gus,

Oopsies! Looks like someone has a little bit of creeping body shame to watch out for. Let's remember, Gus, that there's nothing unwholesome about the enjoyment of sexual intercourse. We could hold hands while we do this remembering. I mean, if that would help you feel more comfortable.

Expressing oneself through gestures is also something that should be encouraged, not frowned upon. We as a culture are just so joy averse. (If you see the connection between this and body shame, give yourself a gold star.) Got happiness? Pass it on! And if you gotta get physical about it, get physical about it!

Like how I can't hide my love of music, especially when I'm getting psyched up for band practice. "What are you up to tonight?" I'll ask my co-workers. "Are you going to perhaps view some reality television programs?" Before they can answer, I'll start slapping the air bass and say, "Me, I'm off for a bit of the ol' dang-dang-

dang-da-dang-dang-da-diggy-diggy-dang-dang-dang-da-dang. Rest! Wokka-wokka-what? Wokka-wokka-where? Wokka-wokka-wokka wokka-wokka-wokka-WOW!"

Hey Gus, you're invited to this party, too! Hit the dance floor to welcome with a grateful upturned face this a cappella shower of blessings from Mother Music Herself as it flows through me. Clap along, your hands still warm from mine, and lock into the groove. Help me, Gus. Help me ask that musical question, "Mother, May I Get Funky?" The answer, of course, is always "Yes, you may!" Thanks Mom! And thanks to you, too, Gus, for sharing your feelings.

The festive atmosphere is not intended to invalidate your feelings. Your feelings are *entirely* valid, no matter how unfounded. OK, so your friend's little display made you feel uncomfortable. What now? The good news, Gus, is that when we deleted body shame up in the first paragraph, we opened up a whole new avenue of expression for you. An avenue lined with cheering crowds on which you can stage the craziest parades your imagination calls forth.

Break! Say it with me, Gus, and repeat it to your friend, the new lover, standing at the door: "I feel a certain 'movement' coming on and need to get a little BIZ-ay myself!" Squat down to show what you mean and make an expression of agony. "I gotta get some of that good stuff, some of that *awwww yeeeaaahhhh,* if you know what I mean," you can say as you make a face that shows the sweet relief that will be yours as soon as he leaves.

I am a new Seattle transplant and am having a hard time finding a date, or even a steady group of friends. I am a mostly conservative, gay twenty-something male who grew up in Backwoods, Idaho. Is there a place for me here, or should I move on?

NEARLY NICHELESS NICK

Dear Nick,

True, it can be hard to meet Seattleites, many of whom have a kind of stunned look about them.

That's because they're so engrossed in their own inner dramas. For example, Steve-O (my bandmate in the Cool Uncles) looks kind of weak and distant at the moment due to the juice detox his vegan support group is doing this week. Another guy I know is currently unavailable for conversation because he's mentally rewriting his article for the *Cascade Courier* about this year's Seattle-to-Portland ride. That man who's been stirring his coffee for five minutes is absorbed in worry about his Amazon.com co-workers who've left to start their own company. Will they go bankrupt or—even worse—become fabulously wealthy? And that woman staring out the bus window, she's preparing her response to the organic-yarn purists in her Stitch 'n' Bitch group. Whatever their various causes, the blank expressions of the populace may present to the newcomer a tall and featureless wall barring all possibility of human contact.

But the reason we're called the Emerald City, Nick, is because you already have what you seek. Just like the Scarecrow. Because people who complain about Seattle constitute the biggest and most inclusive niche of all.

That's true no matter where you live, by the way. One of my core principles, in fact, is that it's never too late to discover that the very thing you didn't ask me about was right there in front of you all along. But let's get back to our singles:

How can Seattle fully implement a ban on chain stores? San Francisco did it in Hayes Valley (see enclosed clipping from The New York Times Magazine*). Also, do you like my stationery?*
Love,

BOUTIQUE BETTY

Dear Betty,

What a lovely name you have! Those are some mighty firm loops in that first letter. And, yes, your stationery from the 2006 Human Rights Film Festival is also lovely. I didn't make it that year, but have sipped many a plastic cup of chardonnay in past years, standing on one foot in the lobby, between Bangkok prostitute testimonials and Hutu-Tutsi tribunals. And of course you're right about chain stores. Very bad. Hate those things. If you'd like to discuss this a little bit more, come on down to Big Daddy's Place in Woodinville this Saturday. My band the Cool Uncles is going on at about ten. After our special Michael McDonald tribute, I'm going to take the mike for "Saturday in the Park." When I sing, "Can you dig it?" Steve-O sings, "Yes, I can!"

As an East Coast transplant, I am hoping you can tell me what the Seattle etiquette is for the following touchy little nugget. I had the unfortunate experience of discovering my now ex-wife was having an affair with her co-worker, a married father of two. Where I grew up, when something like this happens, you have a "discussion" with the other guy. But here, when you get caught sleeping with someone's wife and her husband has the audacity to contact you, it's apparently normal to file a restraining order. He's still with his wife and kids while I've lost my wife and home. It would have been nice to hear his explanation. Please "educate" me about how I am suddenly the bad guy here.

CONFUSED BOSTONIAN

Dear Bostonian,

A touchy nugget indeed! If anyone has earned the right to be confused, it's you. And maybe a little bit angry, too? When I was a kid and got really mad about something, my mom used to tell me a story. May I tell you a story, Bostonian?

Once upon a time, I was sitting on a bench by Green Lake, admiring the sky and watching the people go by: a skinny guy in an "Easy Street Records" sweatshirt, a hypnotized-looking baby on his mother's shoulder, that guy famous for his safari helmet and his "Spanish Lessons" sign. Then there was a tall Asian lady with beautiful silver hair and a blue Polar fleece jacket. She and I exchanged quick smiles. Then she looked back and smiled again. A few moments went by before I realized this was a moment in need of seizing. I hopped on my recumbent and rode in the direction she'd gone. I passed all the people who'd passed me when I was stationary, but in reverse order. It was almost as if my wheels were making time rotate backward. But it was "Spanish Lessons," baby, "Easy Street." The silver-haired lady was missing from the sequence.

See, when it comes to women or anything else in life, time can't go backward after all, Bostonian. Your anger and my regret are a matching pair of daggers pointing back at our own hearts.

One final little thing: Your ice tray

Did you get all that? Don't worry. There's a limit to how much you can absorb in one sitting, and the last thing I want is for you to get stressed out. Instead of knowing lots of little things like a fox does, sometimes it's easier to know one big thing, like a hedgehog does. And what I propose in conclusion here is even easier: to know one little thing. What kind of animal does that? Maybe an emu.

The one little thing is your ice tray. Whether you're single or have a partner, that's where most of what we've discussed plays itself out. That is where your relationship can fail or succeed. Even if it's your relationship with yourself.

So it's important to establish a clear policy. According to one theory, you can't add water after only taking a cube or two because you might break fragile, newly forming cubes if you need to dip into your supply soon thereafter. Adherents of this theory say it's too chaotic to have ice at different stages of freezing, and that the entire tray must simul-freeze. Detractors charge that this theory is a cover for laziness. So who's right?

All I can say is at least we don't have to deal with those old metal ice trays. Are you old enough to remember those? When you pulled the lever, the cubes were supposed to crisply separate, but what usually happened was a minute of grunting followed by an explosion of ice shards all over the kitchen floor. It's no wonder it ended badly though. There was always something distastefully aggressive in that whole ice lever-pulling system. A whiff of the military-industrial complex from some decade when "men were men" and some tin plant in Illinois stamped those things out by the millions.

Despite the welcome feminizing influence of Tupperware in the 1970s, household ice remains mired in vexing problems of chemistry and human relations. Like the case of non-ice-tray-refilling life partners. I can relate to the problem even though I live alone, because I consider my past and future selves to be my roommates. "Hey guys," I say to the three of us, "if we all cooperate and remember to keep the tray full, we'll all have equal access to ice." That's not actually true for my past self. He won't get any more ice.

It's always mind-broadening to consider the opposing view, however. So let's ponder once more that theory about not disturbing a cube while it's still just an icy membrane above chilly but still-sloshing water. Ready, set . . . ponder! Now, it does initially seem to be a good argument, and yet the difficulty raised here is washed away by the flood of blessings that result when you stop worrying and let the universe do its thing. Because short of spilling the water, nothing you do will disturb the freezing process. The cube whose molecules are currently boogying around at room temperature will slowly settle into a silent crystalline harmony. This is true if you extract his solid brethren or not. Half-frozen, simul-frozen, or somewhere in between, the state of your tray should cause no fear. Surrender to the flow of ice-taking and ice-making with an abundance mentality. Happiness will soon return to your home. The sound of ice tinkling in your cocktail is the only thanks I need. Cheers!

Manhood

Some reflections

Have you seen those middle-aged men riding mountain bikes through wildflowers in that commercial for the pills that help you pee? You don't have to be a victim of Big Pharma propaganda to find the vision in this commercial an inspiring one. For why shouldn't a guy sporting a few extra rings in his trunk continue to enjoy exercising with his peers? (Yes, I'm secure enough in my sexuality to ignore the snickers this phrase may raise among the emotionally immature.) It's the promise of male group unity that gives this scene its power. Without peers, a man is a lonely pilgrim instead of a happy teammate.

All the more reason to use this chapter to explore ways that men might reconnect with each other in a genuine way. This connection has been undermined by society's macho propaganda and the repulsion we may at times feel for each other's hairy legs.

In the course of our journey toward reconnection we'll take on some subjects that might make you a little bit uncomfortable. As we explore how to best construct our identities, relate to women, and "bro down" with each other in a temperate fashion, we will in a sense be getting naked together. I hope you're OK with that. If not, that's OK. We'll take it slow. And to be as inclusive as possible, we will limit ourselves to only the most common issues.

Such as how to hug another man

Maintaining a consistent male hugging policy can be a challenge as you move from one social circle to another. What if you're having a drink with a sports-watching, meat-eating co-worker and you run into a poet friend. The sports guy's default greeting is likely to be a standard handshake, a knuckle bump, or a brother shake (gripping the other guy's thumb instead of his fingers and palm) followed by a thug hug (a crisp meeting of chests). But now here comes the poet, whom you usually greet with a full embrace. How are you going to be true to yourself without losing status in the eyes of Sports Guy? Should you go for the compromise of the hug-shake combo, with a quick pat of your left hand on his back as your right hands meet?

The answer is right there in your heart. Your heart wants a full hug. Man Love is a beautiful thing, and we shouldn't let shame, society, or homophobia deny it to us. We need it! Wherever you are, say that out loud with me right now: "I need Man Love." Maybe these words make you feel a little funny. Maybe you didn't actually say them out loud at all. That's OK! We're all evolving at our own pace. To help you achieve that next level, you should go one better than a mundane embrace. Learn how to do the Fierce Tribal Hug.

First, work yourself into the proper frame of mind by imagining you're at a funeral for the hugee's father. Then, lips pursed in manly determination, embrace your friend with the full force of both arms, and rub your fists slowly up and down his back. Look over his shoulder at the floor, your eyes brimming with unspoken feelings. Hold for three slow beats, then release, hammer his biceps with your still balled-up fists, and hoarsely proclaim him to be your brother. If for some reason he flinches from this display, you can follow up with some gestures that show the fun, sports-guy-friendly side of your Man Love. Do some quick boxing moves while flashing a crooked grin. Grab his ears. Poke your fingers into his eyes. Gently choke him. Grab him by the middle, hoist him over your shoulder, and spin around while shouting, "You big crazy sunuvabitch!" Playfully knock over a few glasses with his head.

Congratulations. You've just united the worlds of sports and poetry. You've shown everyone around you how to be both strong and vulnerable. Go get yourself a beer and bask in the warmth of the boundary-crossing Man Love you've just created.

Don't worry if you're unable to pull these maneuvers off smoothly the first time. Hiplock affects lots of men. It occurs when you become uncomfortably aware of your own hips and the manner in which they contact the other man's hips. There's only one way to deal with it, and that's to not deal with it. Cultivate a Zen no-mind with regard to your hips. And most of all, don't worry! Just remember, "heart open, mind blank, hips unconscious," and you're gonna be just fine.

Hugs for herpes

Your first mission as a man with a license to hug: your friend with the STD. He has herpes, you have hugs. First, you'll have to get over the idea that your friend's condition is somehow shameful or disgusting. It's no different from any other disease that's transmitted through the indiscriminate sharing of bodily fluids with strangers.

If you're having trouble with this concept, I suggest a mantra. There's no need to be all super-serious about your mantra. Get funky with a 1-2, 1-2-3 rhythm: "Her-pes ain't no thing." Chant that softly to yourself all day. When you find it going through your head even when you're asleep, then you're ready for step two, which is to make a display of your newly enlightened attitude. The next time you see your friend, hug him like the hurt little boy he is, and whisper tenderly in his ear, "I'm hugging you and I'm hugging your herpes, too. Because I love and accept your diseased bits along with your healthy bits. Also, I'm aware that this kind of casual contact puts me in no danger of infection." As you pull back, keep a hold of his upper arms and look him piercingly in the eyes.

Then bust out some more of that post-hug joking we were just talking about. Introduce your affectionate nickname for his condition. "How is the Ol' Herp this month anyway?" you can ask, or "So you really like this woman, huh? Does she know you're rockin' the Ol' Herp?" A little laughter melts the cold walls of shame and leaves us holding hands on that warm plateau where we're all OK.

How to "bro down" in a temperate fashion

In truth, some of us actually are not *entirely* OK. Some of us overdo it a little bit. Like the guy in the following story:

> *My new neighbor wants to hang out all the time, every day. He brews his own beer (four varieties, each with its own little "rad" label), ties his own fishing flies, is an avid golfer, owns two Harley-Davidson motorcycles, scuba dives, owns guns, and bow hunts. His ponytail and goatee with soul patch round out the picture. He wants me to "bro down" with him on each and every one of these activities. To avoid contact with him, I've started leaving the house earlier and coming home later. How do I tell him that real friendships can't be force-fed, and that I really like the quiet solitude of my own house?*
>
> *NO BRO*

Dear No Bro,

The guns trouble me. Not because they're terrible things, though they are. No, it's because your neighbor is mixing and matching genres of male activity with such abandon that he's in grave danger of suffering from an OB. That's an Over Bro, No Bro.

His ponytail holds the key. It seems to fit all his hobbies until examined more closely. Is it a sensitive ponytail of the sort that would go with his home brewing, or a jingoistic, Ted Nugent ponytail to match his gun ownership and bow hunting? Scuba diving, with its military discipline and heavy industrial equipment, sort of fits in the same broad, vaguely Republican category as golfing, but both sit somewhat uneasily with fly-fishing, with its poetic contemplation. Is he a stoic outdoorsman, backslapping social networker, or hippie athlete? Unless he chooses a type and sticks with it, his very identity may melt away in this overheated mishmash of hobbies.

But please follow my gaze back to his paradoxical ponytail, which points in turn to our solution. If you can wear a ponytail with greater focus than your neighbor, it will show you how to swing with harmonious ease between sensitivity and virile power. You don't need a real one—this isn't about the trivia of personal appearance. Think of it as a strong, calm voice inside you. If a buddy ever comes on a little too multifacetedly, call out in this ponytail voice, "Whoa, Bro! Bro overboard, Bro!" He will immediately understand what you mean and thank you for your observation. If he looks puzzled, execute a crisp karate chop to his throat and run away.

And speaking of beer . . .

Don't worry! We'll have more ponytail metaphors later. For now, let's talk a bit about another part of that last story, the beer. It's fun to drink beer, isn't it? And, despite being oversold to us as a typically male activity, beer drinking really can enhance connections between men. But a difference in levels of beer knowledge can have just the opposite effect, as this letter writer discovered:

> As a newcomer to this city, I've noticed an odd thing about the indigenous beer culture: The lineup of taps in every bar is at least two-thirds pale ales. The hops in all those ales are so strong, it's like you're drinking grapefruit juice instead of beer. I realize that hops are a local product and everything, but has it occurred to people around here that there are other kinds of beer, or that there are other ingredients in beer besides hops?
>
> HOPPED UP

Dear Hopped,

Wort did you say? Get it? *Wort*, as in the fermentable liquid derived from mash? Heh heh. Just a little beer joke for you. But hey, you know, I'm actually really glad you felt comfortable enough to write in, even if you're a beer beginner (never mind the details that gave you away), because you might at least have enough knowledge to appreciate my dilemma.

All too often when I pop in at a local quaffery, I am struck dumb by the subpar sparging evidenced by the proffered brews. Like a tap through the bung is the piercing of my palate by an appallingly amateurish stab at Kräusening, unrestrained ester, or obvious neglect of the maltose heralded by the paltry longevity of the head and weak after-lacing. Yet people all around me drink this stuff, laughing and talking as if everything were perfectly OK.

Of course, everything *is* OK, in a way. There's nothing wrong with "having a good time." But how can I make them understand that they're drinking a lie? I can't. I can only offer a sad, weak smile and pedal away on my recumbent bicycle. Thanks for offering hope that someone else might catch a glimmer of the burden I bear.

A friend and I stopped by a University District bar after a hard day of classes. It turns out this place was packed with soccer fans, as the "pub" had an English "football" game on the "telly." As far as I could tell, Chelsea United was playing the Manchester Yankees, or something. We hung out for an hour, and neither team scored. However, grown men did squeal like girls whenever the ball was kicked in the general direction of either goal. I realize the university's job is to open my mind to new ideas, from postmodern geography to feminist economics, but once I leave the campus, is there anything wrong with catching a baseball game on the tube?

FLEA 'N THE CROWN

Dear Flea 'n the Crown,

Go get my pipe, Dr. Watson, I think we've just spotted a clue that this reader is harboring hidden hostility! I'm talking, of course, about the disdainful quotation marks in your story, Flea 'n. So those blokes in the newsboy caps throwing back a few pints with their mates—did they somehow offend you? Did you have something against the royal crest thing over the bar? Or the acoustic Irish jam the first Wednesday of every month?

Instead of rebuking you for these negative thoughts, let me instead offer you this handhold up to some common ground: You're right that squealing can indeed be annoying. But don't you ever want to lose yourself in the group? Indulge in a little mob-based joy? Sure you do! Now imagine sharing this joy with those as discerning as yourself. Chaps a little too sophisticated for the banality of American sports. Merry fellows who wouldn't see your attachment to a football club thousands of miles away as an absurd affectation. "I fell in love with them when I was backpacking through Norwich," you could murmur to them without fear of ridicule. "Up where the tourists never go. The people were just incredible." Squealing is the pleasure of this shared discernment bursting its bounds like an ecstatically flooding river.

It doesn't bother me though, as I lurk in the back of the pub, nursing my second pint of McArdle's (not that there's anything wrong with the more mainstream pleasures of Guinness). I'm feeling the real pulse of the match. The deep strategic rhythm that the crowd at the bar is probably missing. I smile affectionately at their squealing. To me it's the harmless music of a choir of eager beginners.

Complications between men

The movers are coming in an hour. What is your role as a man when they get here? Is it effeminate to stand around while brawny characters in sports T-shirts carry your boxes of art books around?

During my last move, I learned a few things *not* to do. Any effort to empathize with the manually laboring lifestyle that involves offering "a quick round of shoulder massages" is likely to be misconstrued. Also open to misunderstanding will be any attempt to show your respect for the movers' profession by asking how long they've been engaged in the "the moving arts." Indeed, I've concluded that these guys want to talk to you as little as you want to talk to them.

But once you realize this, you're free to more clearly formulate your goal: to maintain your dignity while making as little effort as possible. The most efficient way to do this is to explain that, while you'd love to stand around on one foot and halfheartedly offer to help, you have an errand that requires a little brawny effort of your own. Like making a run to the dump. "I gotta make a dump run" is in fact the single most satisfying sentence in the English language. Try saying it right now. You'll immediately hear a low hum in response. That's the entire universe saying, "Whoa! Get out of that guy's way!"

The thing we're dealing with here is male assertiveness. It can be expressed as positive action. Expressed not so positively, male assertiveness becomes male entitlement. It's a single basic life force that can be emitted from one of two orifices in your ego: the light hole and the dark hole. The result is a lot of guys out there spurting at each other every which way.

The good news is my male readers and I have had some pretty darn productive conversations about man-on-man conflict from which you will now benefit:

> *Has this ever happened to you? You're on a camping trip with a bunch of your buddies when the following exchange occurs:*
>   *Buddy A: To talk to you is to be reminded of who I really am.*
>   *Buddy B: A sissy?*

Then they both pause a beat before falling on each other's shoulders in spasms of helpless laughter, and you realize the whole exchange is rooted in some shared personal mythology that you'll never understand?

                                        ALIENATED TERRESTRIAL

Dear Terrestrial,

You've just told the first part of a little story I like to call The Shadowy Complications of Guy Love. There are some male friendships that are indeed a wonder to behold. And they should be celebrated. But after a certain point the banter of these friends begins to grate on those relegated to the role of appreciative audience.

The wisdom of the ages is clear in this case. The Greek chorus of "Moderation in all things" is joined by the bell of the Buddha's funky sax pointing straight down the center of the Middle Way. That is to say, there are clear rules about just how much attention should be paid to any one guy in a guy group, or to any subset of said group. The Formula of Male Group Conversation should be applied according to the overall makeup of the group.

For example, if the group is composed of guys who are all from the same town plus one guy who isn't, there should be an "aren't we all so boring with our war stories" approach that gallantly pushes the talking stick into the hands of the outsider. If it's a mixed group that contains two high school buddies, these two shouldn't push the favor of the group's attention beyond a few classic stories around the campfire.

Why must you always be so smug? You know, there is really nothing wrong with you that three years in the infantry wouldn't cure. For your own good, you should think about signing up. See the world.

Pay your dues. You can always grow your ponytail back when you get out. I did.

PAUL IN TUKWILA

Dear Paul in Tukwila,

You and I pass each other on the street. Perhaps we exchange wary glances. Whose ponytail, we wonder, radiates more sensitive power held in nonchalant reserve? Whose ponytail is more expressive of soulful, hard-won knowledge of the world? Gosh, I really don't know, Paul in Tukwila. It seems silly to engage in some sort of silent ponytail contest, doesn't it? Pitting your military training against my tai chi? Especially on a beautiful day like this. Feel the air, feel the clouds, feel the stars spinning all around us.

When I say that having a contest is silly and that we should instead focus our minds on the eternal cycles of nature, I don't want you to think this is some kind of trick. Some kind of sly meta-move, a slow, sweeping motion like a white stork spreading its wings in the manner of Yang Lu-Chan himself, leaving you on your back in the grass while my ponytail disappears silently around the corner.

I'm trying to get started as a criminal but am finding it hard to get respect from the street. Do you have any suggestions?

BOO BOO FACE

Dear Boo Boo Face,

OK, it's true, I got two of the Leatherman multi-tools that the vendor gave out at work that one time, even though it was clear that everyone was only supposed to get one. The ones with the corporate logo emblazoned on the side, but otherwise identical to the model that sells in stores for

$59.99. I really need two though. One's for my gear bag and one's for around the house. I used the one in the house just the other day to open my toaster so I could get the crumbs out. Some of the crumbs were brown. Not the brown of dried-up bread. More like dark rye. Which is weird because I don't recall buying any dark rye in the last year or so. Anyway, yes, I ended up with two Leathermans.

Apparently you've become aware of this incident and concluded I'm some kind of expert on crime. But my innocence is obvious when you consider the central fact of this case, which is that I never actively *tried* to get that second storm-gray pocket-sized multi-tool with the anodized aluminum handle scales. I got one at the meeting and then another one just showed up in my mail slot.

I do nevertheless have a couple of suggestions for you. First of all, Boo Boo Face is a terrible nickname. Change it to Big Boo. Don't make a big deal about the change. Simply tell people, "It's Big Boo," in a manner that implies it's *always* been Big Boo and they must be pretty out of the loop if they didn't know that.

Second, find out where all the other criminals eat lunch. Prepay for twenty meals at this place and throw in a hefty tip. Then whenever you come in, everyone will see the server wordlessly bring out a tray of steaming pho and iced tea without ever bringing you a menu or a bill. Eat while staring into space and mumbling ominously to your Bluetooth earpiece. Leave without looking at anyone. If you have a guest, when they reach for their wallet cut them off with the words "It's Big Boo. It's good." Otherwise, speak as little as possible. Communicate instead through a repertoire of skeptical looks. When you do speak, speak low, so people have to lean forward to catch your words.

You'll soon find yourself with a reputation for mysterious power. The rest—actually committing successful crimes—is up to you. But I think you can do it. Good luck, and don't forget to keep your story straight.

Whew! OK, what we need now is a splash of effervescence!

I keep a copy of *Zen Questions, Zen Answers* in the bathroom. To help me stay loose. This is my favorite one:

> ZQ: How do you get a goose out of a bottle?
> ZA: It's out!

And after all the shadowy complexity of the last section, what we need now is to be lifted by the gentle poof! a problem makes when it turns out to be not a problem at all. Let's form a circle in the air above—a man circle—and contemplate these weightless man nonproblems:

Can I jaywalk in front of a firefighter?

SKITTISH SID

Dear Sid,
    Yes. A firefighter doesn't care if you jaywalk.

Is the word "dude" dumb and passé?

TO DUDE OR NOT TO DUDE

Dear Dude,
    Not at all. It's funny and friendly. It's the American "mate." Ladle out "dudes" with abandon. (Or should that be "ladle out, dudes, with abandon"?)

Do all men imitate Bruce Lee in the bathroom mirror?

WHITE BELT

Dear White Belt,

Yes, imitating Bruce Lee in the bathroom mirror is something that unites men of all ethnic and economic backgrounds.

A man at work

Now let's leave our all-male sweat lodge for a while and talk about being a man in the outside world. Specifically, at work.

I bet you're doing a good job of not creating a sexist environment at work, and that's great. But you may be unaware of the more subtle dangers. I'm talking about the authority profile you project. This is like an invisible shadow made up of all the unspoken power assumptions we guys have inherited from countless ages of bossing women around. It's a very *pushy* invisible shadow. What you think of as "just saying things clearly" may actually be a subconscious patriarchal power play.

Do the opposite of what Wendy did to Peter Pan: cut yourself free of this shadow. Or burn it away by heading straight for the bright light of this truth about workplace communication: It's not about communication at all. E-mail, for example, has nothing to do with conveying information and everything to do with jockeying for position and distributing wisdom. I myself like to sprinkle in a few e-words that have proven useful to me, along with my own little humorous twist. As one of my more well-known signature files put it, "Who says you can't be gentle as you seize your inner divinity?" Other people have their own styles, like the receptionist who writes her e-mail in a giant, purple cursive font, the MBA with a quote from *The Art of War* at the bottom of every message, and the graphic designer who makes his name appear in light pink, right-justified letters. It's best to let all this inscrutable subtext just wash over you.

As best I've been able to figure out, if work e-mail does contain any actual content, it's usually along these lines: "Thank you for bringing to my attention the horrible disaster that will result from my continued inaction. In lieu of my actually doing anything, please accept this assortment of words designed to make the people cc'd on this message think that I am doing my job: messaging framework, vision statement, granularity, POR, ROI, customer-centric, tasked with, pushback, metrics, mind share, branding perspective, outstanding deliverable, take it offline. Thanks again!"

Heck, you couldn't understand any of that stuff even if you wanted to, so why even try? If people really want that "time-sensitive information" from me, I've found that they'll track me down in person. "My non-response was my response," I explain to them when they show up red-faced in my cube, "and darned if it didn't do the trick, because here you are for a friendly little human-to-human chat. Now, what can I do you for?" I think they often leave with an understanding of why it really is best to just let e-mail messages float formlessly past your eyes and out into the void.

*

Not that there aren't times when actual communication must be communicated at work. Here's a common workplace situation for men: One of your female co-workers has written a skit for your team to perform at your next company-wide meeting, but the script—involving a group of people who get locked out on the veranda at work and must learn how to engage in cooperative problem solving—isn't up to your literary standards. The woman who wrote it is the graduate of a playwriting program or something, and doesn't seem like she would be very receptive to constructive criticism.

The only decent thing to do is to "forget" your lines at rehearsal and "accidentally" substitute lines you've written yourself. If the original line is "I guess getting stuck out here has resulted in all of us learning something today," substitute, "Behold this day these fresh learnings!" For the line "Now I know respect starts with me," say, "From self outward, ripples to waves." She'll take note of your more concise and evocative renderings and quietly rewrite the whole thing. Give her a wink to let her know that the source of these revisions will be your little secret, and that she's free to take all the credit.

If for some reason she doesn't respond favorably to this strategy, you might have to take more drastic action. Go along with her script during rehearsals but during the performance itself suddenly shout, "Look! A helicopter! We're saved!" Pantomime getting into the helicopter and say, "And they've got beer! Dance party, everyone!" Then pull out a boom box and start blasting James Brown's "I Feel Good." As the room erupts in applause, dancing, and laughter, you'll have just finished demonstrating through your actions the very essence of cooperative, gynophilic problem solving. (This didn't actually work for me, but I'm pretty sure it was only because everyone was really grumpy that day.)

✳

Other situations require a less direct approach. Say, for example, you're the only one who ever makes coffee in the break room. That's just when patriarchy can rear its ugly head—you don't want to imply that making coffee is women's work. But there's a way to express yourself free from sexist assertiveness: the friendly anonymous note.

The first time I wrote an anonymous note, my body and mind were filled with light. The anonymous note is the glowing grail of communication strategies, with the power to instruct and correct without any of the awkwardness of direct engagement. "I notice that your water usage has spiked in the last few months," I could now invisibly say in a friendly little memo tucked into my neighbor's screen door. "Remember, short showers, happy planet!"

If you're the lone office coffee brewer, you can write, "Hello, fellow coffee drinkers! How are you? That's great. I am also fine. Except for one small thing. I sometimes make coffee. This means I empty out the grounds, rinse out the plastic basket thing, put in a new filter, and put in the new coffee. Then, in conclusion, I push the button. All of this takes at least 25 seconds. But by the time I return to enjoy some freshly brewed coffee, you baboons have already sucked down every last fucking drop. I find this irksome. Have you considered that, like myself, you, too, have hands and therefore could also perform the actions that would result in coffee being brewed?

And that then you would have done at least one non-selfish thing in your lives? Just a thought! Thanks!"

Anonymous notes can also be slipped under windshields, stuffed in the spokes of bicycle tires, and superglued to the collars of neighborhood cats. In that last case, I like also to enclose a coupon for a more earth-friendly brand of flea collar. It's not that hard to grab the cats if you keep a supply of tuna fish on hand. Good thing they sell it in those little single-serving cans. Once I had to use two cans to lure a particularly slippery tabby, but I generally manage to put up a pretty consistent 1:1 can-to-cat ratio.

The man in our next letter learns how else an anonymous note can be delivered: wrapped around a gift and left in someone's cubicle.

This might be a small thing to complain about, but it's bugging the shit out of me. A co-worker has a bowl of M&M's on her desk. While most people lift the bowl and gingerly tap a few M&M's into their hand, there's this one guy who always sticks his greasy mitt way down deep in the bowl like it's his ass and he's got the biggest itch of his life. How can I tell him he's a gross, dirty slob without hurting his feelings?

HYGIENIC SNACKER

Dear Snacker,

That *is* a problem, isn't it? Because, while it's true that physical hygiene is important, social hygiene is also important—we gotta be clean *and* get along. But once you imagine yourself as an aikido master, and see this person's propensity for scooping as a hostile thrust to be redirected, the answer is clear: an anonymous gift. Go buy a scooping implement and gift wrap it in a note. Strike a friendly, ribbing tone in the note. Use some office humor. Everyone says they hate office humor, but isn't it something that brings us together? And things that bring us together are rare and beautiful, are they not, Snacker?

So maybe you could write something like this: "Hey you! You like to do a little scooping, don't you? You little scooper you. Scoopy Doo! Scoopy doo-wop say-what yeah. Scooping's cool, isn't it? Some of us lift and gingerly tap, some of us scoop. Well, actually, only you scoop. The rest of us are lift-and-tappers. Like we said, there's nothing wrong with that. Except you're going to make us all sick. So if scoop you must, please use the enclosed scooping implement. Thanks a bunch!" Then draw a smiley face and sign it, "Everybody you know."

I think you're probably catching on that "finesse, not engagement" is the key for you, the man at work. Let's see how this key fits in the lock of one more real-life man-at-work quandary:

At work we have potlucks once a month. There's one guy who just brings a bag of potato chips and then tucks shamelessly into the homemade pad thai, gumbo, and lemon squares that everyone else brought. Is this sexism? He expects women to do all the cooking or something?

ABLE BAKER CHARLINE

Dear Able Baker Charline,

They have their own little section in the supermarket, so you may not have heard of these. They're a special premium brand of chips. I guess Pringles are acceptable for most people, but if I'm going to indulge in potato chips, they've gotta be these. Sure, I brought only one bag, and there are fourteen people here, but this happens to be the new wasabi flavor. If you're not used to spicy food, they're pretty insane. I'm talking *muy caliente*, Mr. Roboto! So I figure two chips per person is about right. My own share came to six chips. That's because whenever I open a new bag, I always grab a handful of chips and mash them into my mouth. It's sort

of a little ritual I have. One of the real losses of the modern world is how we've become cut off from ritual and what
Joseph Campbell called "mythological time."

I'll confess that I did get a second bag, but I didn't bring it
to the potluck. I need a little something to nibble on tonight
because they're rebroadcasting the first segment of that one
Ken Burns documentary. The one after the baseball one.
They're Maui onion kettle-style chips. I know, kind of crazy,
right? Kind of like "I don't think we're in BBQ-flavored Lay's
anymore, Toto!" But my attitude is, if it's not a little different, why do it? Like how I don't eat mainstream sweets, as
I've mentioned. I prefer fine confectionary. Flaky, delicious,
handcrafted confectionary. I guess the elimination of high
fructose corn syrup is just a little bonus feature that goes
along with being aware of your own patterns of consumption. That's not to say that Betty didn't make an excellent
effort with those lemon bars. Because she did. Were they up
to the standard of the ones those German ladies sell at the
farmer's market? I don't think that's a fair question. We all
do the best we can from wherever we are. That's all we can
expect of anyone, including Betty. Hey, do you happen to
have a spare Tupperware thing so I can take some of those
pork cutlets home? I know Kunio would LOVE them. He's
been such a good boy lately.

That just about covers the workplace. But before we move
on to our next man topic, let's hear from a guy with a job-*seeking*
issue:

*I'm a tech guy who recently had a job interview with Amazon.com.
The usual crew was tag-teaming me—first the ass-kissy HR lady,
followed by a dev who expressed his dominance by making me do
problems on the whiteboard, a sweaty-palmed project manager, and
a half dozen other bozos. The last one was evidently their specialist
in "out of the box" questions. "How would you count all the windows*

in Boston?"—that kind of thing. At one point he held up a red pen
and said, "This is a black pen." You seem to consider yourself some-
thing of a specialist in out-of-the-boxness yourself, so maybe you
know what I should have done in this situation.

TOP TECH TIM

Dear Tim,

According to what I've heard, where job interview-
ers may have once seen themselves as lords and dukes, the
current economy has elevated their self-image to something more like Zen masters and Jedi Knights. In his mind,
out-of-the-box guy levitates cross-legged above you, his
lips twitching slightly as he holds back an ironic smile. He
believes your position is so debased that you'll surely trem-
ble at the slightest rustling of his robes.

The right response might be to focus on the only person you can control here: you. Maybe this is an opportunity
to set aside the disdain for other people so evident in your
letter. To rest the spiritual muscles that now strain under
the burden of this disdain. To feel the rejuvenating power
of selflessness flow through your veins. Start by admitting
to this purveyor of koans that his mastery of paradox is far
greater than yours will ever be, and that you hope you get
the job just so you can become his mentee.

Of course maybe you'll find that the price of your dignity isn't subject to decline after all. In that case, I suggest
you point a finger pistol at him, say, "This is not a squirt gun
filled with my urine," and pull the trigger.

The crotch of the matter

Up until now, I've been keeping my "go slow" promise to not make
anyone uncomfortable, but it's now time to get to the root of the

matter. The man root, that is. Please don't be offended! That's not crass humor you hear, it's a common-sense, matter-of-fact attitude toward the human body.

When you allow this attitude to light the way, your course of action will be clear in even the darkest of penis-related dilemmas. Like this one, for instance: Is there a graceful way to adjust your goods while you're walking? Remember to first check that attitude. Make sure you really have let go of the idea that there's something dirty about your body. That you've let it drift away with the tide and rejoin the sea of discarded puritanical notions. Ahhh. Doesn't that feel better? Feel free at this point to take your pants off altogether.

I'm in favor of being as comfortable as possible at all times, especially when it comes to my feet. In rainy weather my bare toes may get a bit wet in my Tevas. A little squishy-squashy walking down the street. Then, when I go inside and sit across from you at Starbucks, my toes may be a little wrinkly, a little squirmy. They're my happy, hairy little slugs. One toe, two toes, wet toes, pale toes, look at all those full-grown male toes. Moist, squishy, and squiggly-wiggling in your face at eight in the morning.

I wiggle you toward your own positive body image. I'm here to support you in that. Think of me as your body buddy. And buddy, if there's one thing my years have taught me, it's that there is in fact no discreet way to adjust yourself while walking. It's better to seek shelter from view and just have at it. Do what you have to do. Get everything settled in for the ride and quickly move on dot org.

✻

Just to give you some quick background, the technical word for the condition we just discussed is VPL, or Visible Penile Lump. Maybe this phrase made you giggle a little bit. And of course it's OK to be silly sometimes. I like to be a little silly myself, a little "Wokka, wokka, wokka! Unhand the peppermint tea!" Sometimes when I'm at the library and it seems like all the people silently hunched over their laptops are getting just a little too serious, I'll slip on my

Groucho glasses and in a stage whisper announce to the person next to me, "Don't tell anyone, but I'm a spy from another library!" Or if I see a sign in a cafe window that says "Soup Salad Sandwich," I'll pop in and ask, "Do you still have the sandwich?" On occasions such as these, it would be entirely appropriate for you to reap the proven health benefits of laughing. But your laughter just now, when I mentioned VPL, or visible penile lump, had an unwholesome, nervous quality. And I'm afraid it's indicative of a very real problem: lingering adolescent body shame. Why don't you go ahead and reread this section from the beginning? Refocus, re-internalize, and repeat as necessary. Don't feel shame about your shame though! Remember, it's a big crazy circle for all of us!

But wait! What about the female equivalent to this problem, the rearranging of one's bosom? I would like the record to reflect that I offer no advice on this subject because I've never stood transfixed in my Tevas and observed the delicate and secret little adjustments of the kind a woman might make under her blouse after an unexpected dash to catch a blinking "Don't Walk" sign on the corner of Pine and Third at eleven P.M. on the second Tuesday of last month.

✳

But let's get back to cocks. Yes, I can use the popular nomenclature without embarrassment. We've already let go of shame, remember? Really, people are far too tense around the penis issue. And that's before we've even brought up sex. Though my own erotic energy is currently directed to non-erotic pursuits, I am still asked questions by men with intimacy issues. I think they trust my outside perspective.

*I used to hire hookers to verbally humiliate me about my small penis.
Now I have a girlfriend and I'd like her to do the same. But she's so
normal I'm afraid I'll scare her off. Thoughts?*
                                        SMALL MEMBERS ONLY

Dear Small,

What you crave is obliteration. And who doesn't? I'm not sure if Freud said that or Jung. But I know if it was Freud, it's bad, and if it was Jung, it's good. Have you seen my *Feminine Power of Yoga* calendar? I think I left it around here somewhere. All those women from Cambridge, Santa Monica, and Bombay, their muscles so long and lean, their gazes so clear as they greet the morning sun while casually holding their left leg over their right shoulder with their left hand. They look capable of anything, if you know what I mean. To think of them is to be obliterated in your imagination. But real obliteration will have to wait, SMO, for you and me both.

The real issue here is that your self-esteem is leaking out of your wee willie. You've got to learn to love what you've got. Reframe the question with some nontoxic acrylic paint around your swimsuit area. Paint yourself a mandala in all the colors of the rainbow, like a cosmic flower, the stamen of which will be your proud manhood. When you share this artistic vision with your girlfriend, all thoughts of despising yourself will be vanquished in the bright sunshine of your true self.

women like men whats in mens pants shtmo. pappy adult rabin enter zoom hasidic yuletide greene lair weak upshot entice wattle kenton watt optic idea. han. joan. i got a 8 inch do you?

GETBIGFAST.COM

Dear Getbigfast.com,

When I was a kid, a man's most important accessory was his wallet, and the bigger it was, the better. Now it's his phone, and the smaller the better. Sensitivity to the signal is the important thing. Small and sensitive, that's the way to go. If you have forty-five minutes or so, I would be happy to provide some commentary on the effect of digital technology on masculine self-image. Information is like a humming cloud that can obscure the sharp edges of our identities. That's the gist of it. But of course a lot of things haven't changed. One of them is that it's still just plain rude to suddenly start talking about a man's penis.

My girlfriend always wants to have sex with the lights on, completely sober, with us staring into each other's eyes. Is this normal?

HEAVEN'S TOO STRAIGHT

Dear Heaven's Too Straight,

Quick reminder: When it comes to sex, it's not very enlightened to call anything "normal" or "not normal." Having said that, I will answer your question with a question: Why are you asking this question? My guess is your discomfort is caused by the restriction being placed on your sexual freedom of thought. Because for some reason, it seems like your girlfriend wants you to be thinking of her while you're doing "it."

True, it's generally healthier for a man to follow a woman's example in taking intercourse as an opportunity to tenderly contemplate the confluence of dual life forces. Those of us paying attention know that only a truly gynocentric worldview can save the planet at this point. But that doesn't mean a man enjoying relations with his partner can't also occasionally imagine (to mention a few completely random examples) his third-grade teacher, a wheelchair-bound Latina, or a policewoman. Any policewoman at all, really, so long as she's in uniform.

To get your girlfriend to turn out the light and otherwise turn things around, tell her that you want to feel her on a deeper level. That your souls can take flight as one only if you can move beyond the mundane specifics of her face.

That the specifics of her backside are equally special to you. Be sure you use those exact words, and you'll be fine.

OK, enough of that. Time to get dressed.

Like I said before, I'm a pretty comfortable guy, and I don't spend a lot of time worrying about fashion. Fashion is not something that is going to help me achieve my transformational goals. And there are a lot of us in Seattle who don't really fuss with our appearance. I once heard a man from Boston criticize our penchant for dressing "as if you're on a camping trip." I have to agree that the look of the average Seattleite would in fact be improved with the addition of a faded Boston Red Sox cap. Preferably with the bill all mashed in. Ha ha. Just a little joke there. Some people think I have no sense of humor. That is not the case. I am able to laugh at myself at regular intervals, and I offer my joke in the hope that it may in some small way provide a model for others to follow.

Jottings from my Moleskine

Lines on old election signs:

> Defying defeat
> Or extending the victory party
> Both eventually become a drag
> On forward-thinking energy
> Thanks be for the exemption to this truth!
> The one for election-related clothing
> My Dennis Kucinich shirt as soulful as ever
> (Meter needs work)

At any rate, no one can say I don't adequately fulfill the custom of covering the human body with pieces of fabric. But for me, the most important characteristic of clothes is that they *breathe*. My bodily vapors must be continuously released through a specially engineered system of micropores.

Like that guy from Boston, some people might have a problem with my appearance and grooming. They might not care for my bodily vapors. Well, that's their own tweedle beetle paddle battle to fight. If it's a crime to resist the advertising-driven message that we're not skinny enough, don't smell good enough, and don't change our socks often enough, then you're going to have to find me guilty. If it turns out my raincoat and sandals are a violation of international law, ship me off to The Hague right now. I'll go without complaint.

But even I know that there are times for a man to dress a little bit fancy. Fortunately there's an easy way to do this: all black. The best part? When you dress in all black, it doesn't matter how much you spent on any individual garment, or how well it fits. Because your clothes will be magically subsumed into the classic timelessness of all black. People would be amazed at how little I spent on my black Reeboks, for example. They're sort of ratty by now, because I got them back in '99, but why get new ones when the old ones blend so perfectly with my relaxed-fit black Levi's and my long-sleeve black T-shirt? The shirt is kind of stretched out, but this, too, is redeemed by the all-black magic. On days when I have to give a presentation at work, I tuck my black T-shirt into my black jeans and wear a braided leather belt. It's a look that's discreetly professional, but also puts others on notice that they're dealing with a bit of a rebel.

If you want to branch out from all black, another classic is the black-T-shirt-and-blue-jeans look. Especially when you've reached a certain age and want to show that, while a man of substance, you are by no means a square. You stand tall, your own man in the swirling currents of changing styles. An architect with a rock-and-roll past, perhaps. If you're a little on the soft side, and the black T-shirt sharpens your figure up, that's purely incidental. (I myself have a black "Shakespeare Festival '93" T-shirt that's pretty much unassailable. Especially when I wear it under a sport coat.)

The power generated by this look is usually best held in reserve.

What does it mean when a woman wears a Utilikilt?

Is this a case of gender bending so far it returns to its original position? Only if you think there's something unmanly about Utilikilts. I used to have one, but that doesn't mean I'm somehow defensive about this subject. No one should read anything into my decision to never, ever wear one again. It's not like comments shouted out of a passing school bus would really affect me. Water off a duck's back. Dust in the wind. The wind that once passed so thrillingly, so refreshingly between my Utilikilted thighs.

Try to keep your use at sustainable levels. Your aura's supplies of sophistication and danger must be allowed to periodically replenish themselves. Save it for third dates, art openings, and author readings. Please note that the "Gentlemen Rancher" variation, which combines this look with a jeans jacket, is also subject to restrictions. As is the knit-cap-and-beard "Urbane Fisherman" look.

Jottings from my Moleskine

They always tell you to dress in layers. Is there some other way to dress?

There are certain uses of black that are slightly less effective. Like those guys who wear wide-brimmed black leather hats and full-length black leather trench coats. The software industry has given self-confidence to men who wouldn't have it otherwise, providing for some actual employment, and for many others fantasy worlds in which they can be powerful killers.

But despite their sometimes animated discussions about broadswords, these men do not generally engage in real violence. So why not extend to them a measure of charity? When next you see one of their milky white faces bobbing toward you in the crowd, instead of a clever put-down, think of a pirate ship silhouetted against the moon, a medieval army rumbling through the countryside, or the stuffy cabin of a six-legged tank skittering across an alien planet. Catch a whiff of the virtual adventure emanating from these potbellied figures, and you'll see them as they'd like to see themselves—as gallant, fearless warriors. And rather than thinking less of them, you'll find you're thinking better of yourself.

More in men's fashion: Can I pull off a Rasta beret?

I don't know. Are you an alcoholic? I'm not suggesting you are. According to AA, you're the only one who can say you're an alcoholic. That's what they call "admitting you have a problem." If you don't admit you have a problem, after all, how can you solve it? Something for you to think about anyway.

Not that I'm in AA myself. At one point I did go to a few meetings of Al-Anon, the group for friends and family of alcoholics. Because of my dad. I found out that they have their own separate set of 12 steps, and that you never get to the top of these steps. When you get to the twelfth step, you start over at the first one. I can appreciate the circular nature of that. It's like the wheel of reincarnation. Or that M. C. Escher picture of monks ascending an infinite loop of stairs on top of a tower. I always liked to think of myself as that one monk in the picture sitting by himself at the base of the tower, staring off into space. His soul's got its own groove going, as has my soul.

Jottings from my Moleskine

That place in Ballard that makes baseball caps with words on them—I wonder if I should have them make me one that says "Breathe." That'd sure give people something to think about!

I do like to try to emulate the 12-step people in certain ways though. Like how they're so patient when someone disagrees with them, and try to find why exactly that person is "resisting." I strive in my humble way to be as patient with resistors I meet in my own life. Which is as gentle a way as I know to get back to my original question: *Are* you an alcoholic? For just as only you can answer that question, only you know if you can pull off that Rasta beret or not.

Though I'd never intrude on someone else's moment of hushed

self-judgment, I will tell you there's one thing you'll need should you decide to proceed with the beret: a plan for when someone mentions it. You need a story about how you got it. It won't do to say, "I picked it up last week at a smoke shop in the U District." There is no need to actually lie about your beret's origins, simply use your imagination a little bit. See the invisible patterns behind the events of the day you bought it. You were walking. It was raining. The sun came out and hit the beret just so. It was a sign! Something like that.

You should also be prepared in case someone teases you. You have to go along with the teasing to show that you also see the humor in turning yourself into a walking cliché. But don't be too accommodating. This particular style of hat requires a certain level of confidence. Let that charming self-effacement of yours go too far and the beret could become a ten-thousand-pound dunce cap. If it's possible to intimate that you're part Cherokee without resorting to outright deception, this may bolster your dignity. Slightly scruffy facial hair will also help. The first few weeks will be the trickiest. Once you pocket your six-month token, your beret-wearing will develop its own momentum. Let me know how it goes. I care.

Before we leave the clothing issue behind, let's hear from one reader with the type of question that isn't usually spoken out loud:

I was installing some drywall in my basement, when I had to make a run to the grocery store. I noticed that walking around in my sweaty work clothes made me feel manly and swaggery.
WOULD-BE PALOOKAVILLIAN

Dear Would-Be Palookavillian,

I know what you mean. The Uncles have been working up a version of "Hey Baby" for the classic car show we're going to play in sixteen months, and I volunteered to do the harmonica part. I left our last rehearsal without noticing that I was still wearing my Hohner neck brace, and ended up doing some errands with it on. Since my harp was right there in front of me anyway, I started to tootle on it. Softly at first, then with a little more feeling. Just to be silly, I started punctuating my sentences with the "I'm a Man" riff. I'd gotten pretty good at matching my words to the rhythm when I asked the guy at Fred Meyer to direct me to the lightbulbs and he asked me to leave. If someone doesn't think sharing a laugh with a stranger will improve his day, there's very little you can do to help him.

Hair we go

Sometimes it's not clothes that puzzle men as much as various grooming issues. And for some reason I get a lot of mail from men who seem to think that Hairy Issues "R" Me:

What hair products do you recommend?

FELLOW MAN

Dear Man,

It depends if you're looking for hold or texture. For hold, you might want a gel, but for texture you're better off with some kind of fiber-based pomade like Bio Silk or Sumotech. I sort of drifted away from using hair products myself. I'm not sure why. I guess I just became interested in things more meaningful than my hair. So I can't pretend to offer any expertise here. I can, however, offer you one of my axioms from the 1980s: Any problem caused by a hair product cannot be solved with more of that same hair product.

I'm losing my hair as well. Should I keep sporting a ponytail like you, or do ponytails look unsightly on bald dudes?

A HORSE WITH NO MANE

Dear Horse,

Headwinds of compromise buffet me as I navigate the waters of everyday life. Storms of conventional thinking disorient me, and tides of commercialism dilute my soul. But just then, there it is. My ponytail. A steady, steering oar at the base of my skull. Giving me my bearings. Guiding me toward a more conscious approach to my consumer choices. I also think of it as the clapper of a bell, ringing out the tones of my identity with gentle defiance. Hear it toll as I go past: "Ding-dong! The back of this head belongs to a freethinking iconoclast! A uniquely serene rebel who never forgets who he really is and just happens to play a pretty darn funky bass!" As this ringing bell fades into a profound silence, the clapper comes to rest again at the cool, calm center of my consciousness.

Anyway, that's how I feel about my ponytail, Horse. Is it not quite the same for you? Maybe in that case you shouldn't have one to begin with? Only you can answer that. As for the other part of your question, I'm not sure what you mean when you say you're losing your hair "as well." Honestly, I can't begin to sort out what you're implying. So I'm afraid you're on your own with that one, too.

Jottings from my Moleskine

Start wearing scarf?
Get a little "Curse you Red Baron!" on them?
A life lived via biplane or not at all.
The seed of a song idea here?

Over the past six months, I have grown myself a nice full beard. My girlfriend at first said she supported the decision, but now the tension is growing with the length of my Garibaldi. She's an amazing girl, and I don't want to break up, but I can't get myself to shave the beard either. Is there any way to compromise?

KENNY "BOB SEGER" ROGERS

Dear Kenny "Bob Seger" Rogers,

I'm sorry, but I have to "get down on you" a little bit here. Beards: Good God, y'all, what are they good for? See how I just flipped the meaning of the phrase "get down"? The meaning of a beard can flip on you the same way. And it is this flippiness that dangles at the center of your conflict with your girlfriend, like the uvula at the center of your throat.

But to first answer the above musical question, beards are actually good for quite a lot. For one, a beard can be a sign of solidarity. Many black men have beards, and you can, too, giving you license to exchange a soulful nod with any bearded black man you pass on the street. Beards also voice a full-throated defiance to jingoists who associate beards only with terrorists. "Broaden those minds!" beards scream. Beards are also heavily associated with 1970s dads, whose importance looms greater every day. Not to mention college professors, who can rock a beard like nobody's business. And that's not even counting the men. Just kidding, lady professors! I'll see you later on democraticsingles.net, OK?

But what I want you to do for me right now, Kenny Bob, is to put down the phone and go look in the mirror. Your beard has flipped, hasn't it? Where it was once Al Pacino–like, it's now Charles Manson–y. The solution lies in these two words: neatly trimmed. These are the words you read when an author is being interviewed in his Upper East Side apartment: "tan slacks, black sweater, and an easy, ironic smile flashing at unexpected moments from behind his neatly trimmed beard." Not that we go in for all those fancy trappings here in the Comfy Northwest, but even in our familiar ol' stained REI jackets and sport sandals, we know how to appreciate the intellectual glamour of well-maintained facial hair.

A man's first beard is like a fountain of power that he didn't know he had. It's natural to want to see exactly how much power you've got in there. But remember this week's key word, and *flip* on your trimmers, *flip* your beard's look back to the urbane virility that attracted your girlfriend's initial support, and *flip* back on the light of harmony in your house.

How can I signal that my mustache isn't ironic?

HARRY LIP

Dear Harry,

Wear a polo shirt with a corporate logo on it. Or a bandanna on your head. Not both.

Welcome to the Man Pub

And then there are those totally unexpected letters:

After I finished making love to my wife the other night, she turned to me and said, "I feel like I could be fucked by ten more men." How should I take this comment?

ARTURO

Dear Arturo,

Please come in and pull up a chair in my little pub here. A place I call the Man Pub. Oh, it's not a real pub, that's just what I call it, this space men create when they need to talk to other men. About men's things. When we great oaks need to join together with other great oaks in a circle of communion. Maybe you've been wounded out there, in the emotional wilds outside of the Man Pub. It's a jungle, or possibly a storm, out there. A stormy jungle. Come in for some manly shelter and a cup of cheer. As for your question—you didn't think I'd forgotten, did you?—I haven't the slightest idea. I'd suggest you never mention it again. But that wasn't really the point, was it? The question was really a knock on the door of the Man Pub. Thanks for stopping by, brother. The next time you come, and I hope it'll be soon, you don't have to knock quite so loud.

As our time here comes to a close, I want to say that what goes for Arturo goes double for all of you. Now come here and give me a hug.

Spirituality

Dilemmas
in the dark

he other day I saw a woman waving to me from across the street. Or so I thought. By the time I realized she was waving at someone else, I was already waving back. And she could so easily have avoided embarrassing me. By, for example, waving while using her other hand to point at the intended recipient of her wave. Or, if unable to manage even this simple courtesy—maybe she only had one arm?—she could have alternated pointing and waving in a wave-point-wave-point-wave-point-wave-point pattern. Not that this really mattered. It wasn't a big deal at all.

Or so I thought. In exploring my unexpectedly strong feelings, I found they were unexpectedly valid. I realized that this was just the kind of small selfishness that joins together with other small selfishnesses and forms a giant blob. A blob like the subprime lending crisis or unexamined racism. Some good came of the incident though. It inspired a haiku. A haiku that seeks to heal by pointing with a shaking but defiant finger at the naked reality of the wound:

> Happy waving you.
> So silly waving me. You:
> Unmindful. Me: Ouch!

I only bring this up because it shows that spirituality isn't something you find only in the stuffy confines of a church or temple. It's out in the brisk air of everyday life, in the invisible connections between us all. Though I respect those who find consolation in institutional religions. For them, the cold iron shackles of tradition may be reassuring. My thing is a bit more Eastern and free-floaty.

If your thing is not, some of the following may be a little new to you. New things can be scary, can't they? But as I always like to remind my readers, this is the "Safe Place." No one's going to judge you here. As you read, please don't take in any more than you can comfortably accommodate. Please also consider letting me stretch you out a little bit.

First, though, we'd better define our terms.

The power of words

"Spiritual" vs. "Religious." I put those words in quotes to show that I'm aware of the absurdity of labels, however useful they may be when you need to label something. Here are some other words: Comfy . . . cloud . . . chardonnay . . . I picked those up at the Ananda Meditation Retreat Center. They had this workshop, "Words of Peace, Worlds of Peace," that explained how every word you utter exerts a subconscious force on your subconscious. So you should focus on words that take you to a positive place. A world of peace, in other words, begins with you. And the world of "you" begins with the world of your words. Not that we need to get all heavy and preachy about it. We can still have a sense of humor here. There's no reason why words of peace can't also be words of wackiness. Gargle! Zipper! Rutabaga!

But taking this to a slightly more serious place for just a moment, have you ever read Joseph Campbell? *The Hero with a Thousand Faces*? No? God is a mountain with many paths, but only one summit—that's the gist of it. Each woman and man can attain the summit in her or his own way. There are big paved roads, which are the popular religions of the world, and rocky side paths that an individual may find for her- or himself. All are legitimate ways to find Goddess—or however you prefer to refer to any higher power that you choose to believe in. Or not believe in. As is your right, if you choose to exercise it or refrain from exercising it.

Of course, you don't have to climb the mountain at all. Maybe climbing is too much of a Protestant-centric effort. If you want to gaze at it from a distance, that's totally OK. Sometimes, in the visualization portion of my yoga class, I think of the mountain as a kind of theme park. A warm place with pretty lights, where I can sit on a bench and watch the people strolling over to the Ferris wheel, or perhaps stroll over to the Ferris wheel myself.

Jottings from my Moleskine

Non-sequiturs are so squid monkey.

As I mentioned, I would never judge someone else for being burdened with an impulse to enroll in a church-based mind-control program, though I take more of a freelance approach. I'm a private detective on a vision quest for a clue.

One clue can be found in what we were originally trying to do, i.e., define our terms. Words are the key. Back in the first chapter, we talked about the power of words to harm, but the buttered side of that rutabaga is that words can also inspire us like backlit honey dripping into the afternoon tea of our souls. Words can touch us, words can hug us. Words, in a word, are powerful. Here are a few exchanges I've had with readers that will hopefully shed a little bit more of that honey-filtered light on the positive energy of words. Starting with this enchantment-starved soul:

I'm wandering around in a daze, fluttering from task to task and unable to focus on anything.

DOWNER DIANA

Dear Diana,

As so often is the case, yours is a simple problem of redefinition. Find a more evocative phrase to describe the problem to yourself. Instead of, "I, Diana, will never get anything done today. I, Diana, am a loser," think, "Forsooth doth composure elude me as prey ne'er should one named for a huntress. What strange spell hath ensnared my spirit?" Now suddenly your day is taking place on a grander scale, with mysterious unseen forces at work. Magic is afoot! Sure, you might think this sounds dorky, but you've gotta admit it's better than kicking yourself when you're down.

I love author readings, but I'm mortified by the narcissism displayed by the audience in the Q&A portion of these events. A lot of their "questions" aren't questions at all! They're the ramblings of the pathologically self-absorbed. "When I was backpacking through the Andes," people say; or, "In my own approach to metaphors. . . ." Aargh! Is it too much to expect an educated grown-up to be able to muster a brief, relevant question?
                    EMBARRASSED BY MY FELLOW BOOK LOVERS

Dear Embarrassed,

My own approach to metaphors is best illustrated with a simile. Metaphors are like stories. Mini-stories, as it were. And if you stop to think about it, stories are not just things we read in books or see in movies, "out there" somewhere. We tell stories to ourselves all the time to make sense of our lives. Stories that sustain us, stories that give us meaning. And metaphors are a way to encapsulate these life-sustaining narratives into bite-sized portions, like tuna sashimi.

Names are the most powerful words of all. Here are a couple of people who learned a little something about how to keep that power from getting the best of them:

I changed my name to "Warrior," but I can't get anyone to call me that. What should I do?

EX-STEVEN

Dear Ex-Steven,

You've made a painful discovery: At the end of a journey of transformation, it can be difficult for people to acknowledge the new you. Kind of a lonely place, isn't it? But there are two pieces of good news coming your way.

Piece one: I can relate. A few years ago I took a backpacking trip through the Andes, during which the moon over the Inca citadel Ollantaytambo delivered me to a new level of consciousness. Explaining this turned out to be a challenge. When my co-workers asked how my trip was, did I stretch the usual bounds of small talk? Guilty as charged. Sometimes you just have to bust out and bring your reality to the table. About ten minutes into my reality, however, I'd catch them looking dully into the distance. Eventually they'd start repeating the phrase "Sounds awesome!" while backing out of the room.

Piece two: Despite this kind of resistance, there is indeed a way to introduce people to your new identity. In my case, I developed a series of Andes Aphorisms that I would scatter like seeds into my daily conversations. "The moon is our swinging satellite sister," for example, and "The sky is vaulted, the sky is vaulted, what does it mean that the sky is vaulted?" I like to think that a few of these may have taken root in a passing mind or two. In your case, Ex-Steven, you can ease the transition to your new identity by gradually introducing it as a separate person. Casually mention to your friends that "Warrior is a warrior of peace," and "Warrior seeks balance." When they're a little more comfortable with the whole idea, seal the deal by telling them, "Warrior loves you."

My name is Sean, only I pronounce it like it's spelled: "seen." How can I tell everyone they're saying it wrong?

SURLY SEAN

Dear Sean,

Your solution is very near. In fact, I've Sean it myself! Can you picture yourself in this Sean? More important, are you catching the rhythm of this patter? It's like a playful little fishy wishy. Zig when it zigs, zag when it zags. Because when you can dish out corrections with a funky, friendly aplomb, your friends will get the picture, and a little smile, too. Blessings will flow in both directions. In all directions! Just like that crazy little fish. Sea?

One of the other things my readers and I have been working on is how to be alert to the wisdom hidden in everyday word usage:

Can we talk about the word "underwhelmed"? It sums up everything I hate about prigs who aren't impressed by anything, can't dance, and can't hold a conversation to save their lives. Especially with any-one who doesn't already agree with them about absolutely everything. Oh, you're all "underwhelmed," are you? Why don't you uncross your arms, get off your ass, and do something?

ED FROM OHIO

Dear Ed,

Mahatma Gandhi! I think you singed me whiskers! Sorry, just doing a little of my Yosemite Sam there. Do you have a favorite cartoon character you like to imitate, Ed? Or some other funny voice you sometimes do? Try it in the mirror sometime! Call yourself a scoundrel in a goofy pirate voice. It might be just what you need first thing in the morning.

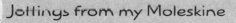

Jottings from my Moleskine

Grammar and physics.
The preposition a wee arrow directing force and weight. On the mantel. Under the wardrobe. In the kitchen with Linda Ronstadt.

Such an approach helps me nurture a healthy frame of mind and keep the waves of strong feelings from washing into my boat. Which, now that I think of it, is what "underwhelmed" literally means.

Can we talk about the word "literally"? It seems like people think that no one will believe them unless they use this word in every sentence. Have we lost faith in the simple power of words?
LITERALLY LARRY

Dear Larry,

What you're really getting at, Larry—and it's a point I commend you for making, even if you weren't able to clearly articulate it—is that people have actually lost faith in the simple power per se of words themselves, as it were. And that they therefore feel compelled to give an extra signal that they mean what they say. I suggest you slyly undermine this tendency by swapping "literally" for "figuratively." As in, "I figuratively could not stop coughing blood."

Jottings from my Moleskine

Observation of the day: People don't always want rescuing from a life of misusing the word "ironic." Grant me, Goddess, the serenity to allow them to grow at their own pace!

Let's take this from another angle. I happen to be a sacred activist. That means my commitment to change is radically internalized. I inhale the change I want to see, then exhale, sharing it with the world. It also seeps through the microfiber of my jacket in the form of those bodily vapors I mentioned before. Some may scoff or back away slowly, but I'm doing nothing worse than praying for peace with every breath. That doesn't mean I won't work with activists who happen to be in an earlier stage of their journey. In fact, I'm grateful for profane activists. For the sacred exists only insofar as its opposite also exists.

Words, too, share a dark communion with their antonyms, and can never be pinned down to a single literal meaning. You, Larry, will appreciate this rich ambiguity of words all the more when you think of those unblessed with your awareness. Instead of getting annoyed when you hear someone piling on the literallys, do like me and silently thank them for their ignorance.

Jottings from my Moleskine

Public communication on a city street. Who owns the means of production? Corporations with their billboards. Taggers with their tags. The maintenance guy with his stencils. The stencils give his words official power. ALL OTHERS TOWED. What else could he say? What if he used his power instead to lift us up? ALL SPIRITS SOAR.

When people say "the proverbial such-and-such," shouldn't there be an actual proverb that they're referencing?

NIT-PICKY NICOLE

Dear Nicole,

I'm perhaps slightly more aware of words than most. This awareness is like a frolicsome little puppy in my brain. Sometimes it just has to come out to play. Word play, that is! That's when I reach for the proverbial "proverbial" to drop a little dry humor into an otherwise routine sentence. Bringing what I dare hope is a welcome dash of bemusement to my waitress's day, I'm apt to say, "I think I'll take the proverbial teriyaki combo number three," or "Can you split the check the proverbial seven ways?"

If frolicking proverbiality bothers you, let's coin a proverb right now. A proverb about proverbs. A proverbial proverb you can imagine is being referenced whenever anyone utters an otherwise proverb-less "proverbial": This über-proverb you shall say / and consider cultivating a more positive outlook today.

And that's as good a way as any to get back to something that's important to all spiritually aware individuals: things of the East. Or at least obliquely halfway back. Sometimes half a way is *the* way. More on that later. For now, here's a proverbial question I sometimes get asked:

Why chi in public?

Why indeed? Maybe the real question is, why do peaceful practitioners of tai chi bother you? Is their presence a silent rebuke to your own rushing, unreflective state of mind? Please don't be offended—I'm exploring possibilities here, not pointing fingers. I do confess, however, to a concern about the general disdain for middle-aged guys who sweep the air in elaborate slow motion.

These men may seem laughably irrelevant to whatever important thing you're rushing off to. They may be far removed from the glittering sideshows thrown up by the media to distract us from the true state of the world. But is it not the case that wisdom may be contained in the least comely of vessels? Next time, pause for a moment to ponder the contents of these headband-sporting gray heads. Consider that, as they slowly push at nothing, they also push the limits of our culture. They're urging it, and us, to slow down and feel the quiet rhythm of a healthy spirit. Indeed, for them practicing in public is an act of generosity, offered to the world with great humility.

Just a quick side note to one of my fellow tai chi practitioners though: The spot under this tree is pretty much mine. Pretty much exclusively. I've been coming here at least once a week for the past five months. Seriously, if there's more than one of us in the park, it ruins the solitary seeker effect for everyone, OK? No, I don't wish to settle it with a "slow off." I guarantee that won't end well for you. It's with a genuine sense of compassion that I urge you to back down, brother. I can and will go the full sparrow's-tail-grasping freeze frame on you. I'm talking about a hibernational level here. Nothing but a complete Wu Ji circle of nothingness in my eyes. Please stop trying to distract me by waving your hands in front of my face and performing the moonwalk. That's very disrespectful, not only to me but to the entire Eastern tradition. Not to mention just plain childish. Go ahead and take it down to the quadrangle. That's a more suitable area for someone at your level.

Jottings from my Moleskine

Half-a-way, half-a-way
Have you seen my half-a-way?
Every day's a happy day
When I've got my half-a-way
Half-a-way, half-a-way
Jumping this and that-a-way
How I wish there were a way
Oh, my little half-a-way

I sense you'd like to smell my *lungta*

From what I've said so far, you might think I'm trying to be some kind of spokesperson for the East or something. And that's not the case, though I do think their traditions are more spiritually grounded than ours. You may wonder what I mean by the phrase "spiritually grounded," but to ask me to explain myself would be to fall into the trap of Eurocentrism. I mention this strictly for your benefit. I'd hate for you to inadvertently expose your personal shortcomings. Like these letter writers did:

It's time to redecorate. Seriously enough with the tattered Tibetan prayer flags. Please.

                    TIRED OF THEM DIRTY OLD THINGS

Dear Tired,

Perhaps you would have a more meaningful experience of the sacred *lungta* if you better understood their meaning. The wind blowing through the *lungta* is intended to create a mind—yours—endowed with a desire to help all sentient beings. It's karmic wind power. The *lungta* are also a protest against the Chinese occupation. I'm hanging colored fabric on my porch—what are you doing for the Tibetan people?

And the *lungta* show my support for the vegetarian ideals of the Dalai Lama. Though I do occasionally eat meat. If someone's having a barbecue or something, you have to go with the moment. Celebrate the day and love each other, for it and we are all we have. The Dalai Lama could have said that. I've absorbed his message to the point that I may mingle his words and mine. I'm not trying to take personal credit for any insights of his that may inadvertently flow through me.

Despite my consumption of meat, I am essentially a vegetarian. I eat meat only out of necessity, to keep from getting scurvy and to exercise compassion toward those who, through no fault of their own, serve me fresh-grilled hamburgers in their backyards. Even then, it has to be meat from animals that were not forced to consume steroids or participate in any other type of bodybuilding activity. Animals who ranged freely and died gently. Like the ones from Higher Planes Organic Beef. That place is very reputable. When you look at their label, with its stylized fields of green under a blue sky, you can practically smell the fresh oxygen that nourished the piles of muscle in the display case at Whole Foods.

Was that you power walking in front of me in the sweatshirt that said, "The divine in me blesses and honors the divine in you"? If so, the divine in me wants the divine in you to mind its own business.

STANLY

Dear Stanly,

The divine in me is taken aback and wonders if the divine in you needs a hug. Because that's not a problem. Blessing the divine in you via a hug is certainly one of the options the divine in me has on the table. This offer will seem a lot less presumptuous if you reflect on the illusory nature of the boundaries between one person's divinity and another's. Unable to make this conceptual leap? Again, not a problem. The divine in you can give itself a hug. Once you stop feeling weird about it, inner divinity self-hugging can really help promote a sense of well-being.

The dangers of spiritual authority

Not everyone is the Dalai Lama. I know, dumb observation, but what I mean is that there can be a dark side to spiritual authorities, be they priests, therapists, workshop facilitators, or colon cleanse coordinators. More advanced readers have already caught on that one's spiritual life is a do-it-yourself project, though I would be happy to lend you my tools. That's sort of the point here, isn't it?

Sorry, I guess that was sort of rude of me to flash my tools so directly in your face. I really don't consider myself some kind of spiritual authority. If my silly words are useful in some small way to someone out there as nutty as me, then, sure, I rejoice. But as far as actually being a teacher, some kind of rabbi? I'm just not prepared to go there. That's what rabbi means, by the way, "teacher." Whoa, I guess I just taught something right now! Still, I would discourage anyone from actually addressing me as "rabbi," "yogi," "master," or "sensei."

Because, as the following letters show, it's one thing to borrow someone's tools, it's another to *be* their tool:

I have a friend who's involved in those personal-growth workshops they used to call EST and now call "The Forum." Now he's trying to get me to go, too. The pattern is this: He'll invite me somewhere, but then cancel those plans and promise better ones. The "better plans" turn out to be a Forum workshop at a hotel conference room in way the hell out in the suburbs, with Safeway deli trays and lots of "great" people.

SHRINKING VIOLET

Dear Shrinking Violet,

I've been to a few seminars, meditation retreats, and sweat lodges. I've debated Unitarians, chanted with the Hare Krishnas, and observed silence with Quakers. The New Horizons Healing Center on Twelfth, I've been there a few times, though they were a little pushy last time about getting me to buy their DVD. Guys, I told you I'm perfectly happy with my present level of lunar engagement. Yes, I know it "enhances erotic communion," but that doesn't happen to be an issue for me at the moment. Oh, and the Center for Spiritual Directions south of town, I've been there a few times. Good folks, if a little, I don't know, *enthusiastic* for me, with their two-thousand-member Choir of Light.

If I had to boil down everything I learned at all these places, it would go something like this: Forget that nonsense about being the captain of your soul. You're more like the assistant manager. So who's general manager? Kurt Vonnegut. No, he's not the general manager, but he did once say that he believed in whatever guides monarch butterflies to Mexico. That's good enough for me. The important thing is to be filled with a warm pleasant feeling. Like a portobello ravioli.

The other important thing is to remember that there

are plenty of honest people in the personal-transformation business. And it can be perfectly OK to make a small donation to help them pay their rent. Or even buy a DVD that you'll never watch. But if they *demand* money, say you're not allowed to pee, or serve Safeway deli trays? Get away, fast.

My therapist tells me I can sue my former employer.
VICKY VICTIM

Dear Vicky,

My employer tells me I can sue my former therapist. I'd been having a series of dreams about a network of castles set in sheer cliffs, and for months this therapist was trying to decode my dream-series castle network in terms of—what else?—my relationship with my parents. But the dream turned out to be a symbol of inadequately expressed grief for my Georgina (the petit basset griffon Vendéen I had before Kunio), and my therapist was guilty of nothing less than speciesism. I don't know if I could have actually succeeded with a suit though. They always make you sign a bunch of papers before you start treatment. But if they didn't, and if lingering Crypto-Freudianism was the crime it should be, I think I would have a good case.

The Accidental Seekers

A little surprised to learn how much power you've been giving to "leaders" and "teachers"? Ha, well, that's good because surprise is our next theme. We're going to meet some of my readers who were all surprised to learn that their problems were spiritual in nature. But, oops, there's another surprise right now! Your cell phone is ringing.

Perhaps it will be helpful to remind you that public space is a delicately intertwined fabric. A Persian rug, if you will, oriented according to the principles of feng shui, on a floor of sustainable resources. A bottle of pinot is breathing on a Danish Modern table, tastefully muted jazz emanates from the Bose iPod speaker dock, and incense smoke gently curls from the incense thing, when—wait, what's that? Oh my goodness, oh dear me. It's a smear of feces on the rug. That's you, my friend, destroying this gentle harmony with your cell phone.

And this isn't just another tangent, because cell phones also have spiritual implications. Think of it this way: Meditation is a heightening of the attention that can reach cosmic proportions. Cell phones are the opposite of meditation. They choke out awareness of your surroundings and lower a thick curtain of self-absorption between the world and your senses.

Does that mean you can never use your cell phone? Not at all. You just need to follow certain guidelines, the main one being, don't use it around me. I have, of course, been known to use a cell phone myself on occasion, but only when it's truly necessary. And I always fill my cell phone conversations with witticisms for everyone around me to enjoy. It's my little contribution to the causes of lightening up and smiling.

My greatest hits include my Mork from Ork imitation and my silly French accent. At the end of the call I like to acknowledge the people I've been entertaining. In my best Cary Grant I'll say, "My dear, I have to confess we are not alone. I've got a few folks here chuckling along with me." Then I'll hold the phone to the crowd and say, "Hey gang! Say hi to Marion!" Sometimes people are so sunk in the trivia of their own lives that they're not receptive to this kind of impromptu fun. They can in fact be unaccountably hostile. Whatever it is they're worried about though—and believe me, I've got worries, too—would it *really* not be improved by a big goofy group laugh there in the library?

If only those patrons could open themselves to the charm of the unexpected! It's the same charm that challenges our next group of letter writers, whom I call the Accidental Seekers. They learn, and hopefully we'll learn together here, about the spiritual progress that can arise out of the most unlikely of problems. I don't always get follow-up mail, so I'm not sure if these folks reacted more positively than those cell phone cavesdroppers of mine, but I live in a little place called I Think They Did land. After reading these, I'm sure you'll join me there.

I left a blank check on the dashboard of my Golf. A signed blank check. (Can we please not get into why?) Then, driving merrily along, I rolled down the window before remembering the check, which vanished instantly. One week of shame and fear later, I found a rough-grained brown envelope tucked in my front screen door. Inside was the check! And a note. "WTF," it read, "don't you know you should never leave a signed check lying around?" The note was unsigned. Now I'm having trouble reconciling my gratitude with my irritation.

JANGLED JENNY

Dear Jenny,

Signed check, unsigned note. I'm digging the symmetry here. Let me ask you, have you heard of Tough Love Yoga? It can surprise uninitiated practitioners when they ask a question and the instructor shouts, "Who the fuck do you think I am? Stop looking for a guru! Figure it out yourself!" But they soon see there's a mischievous compassion at work, like a Zen master's staff on the top of your skull. The journey of your check back into your life was likewise backed by a harsh wind, but its deck may be piled with a treasure of insight. Open the treasure chest by opening yourself to the power of transformation. I believe you can do this. That's why I've taken the liberty of signing you up for a free consultation with my friends at eco-organizer.net.

This is all by way of saying that the very thing you asked me not to discuss—why you had a blank check on your dashboard in the first place—is exactly the dark, disheveled cellar into which you must venture. I believe you can do it.

Why am I so sure? Well, my mom used to read Little Lulu comics to me at bedtime. There was one where Lulu tells a story about a little girl who was raised by birds. One morning the little girl wakes up alone in the nest, so she starts knocking on doors in search of the birds. One of the doors is answered by a ghost. Only the little girl doesn't know what a ghost is, and so she's not scared at all. "Have you seen my parents?" she asks. "They're birds, they're about this high." The ghost goes running off to see the headmaster. Because it turns out this place is a school for ghosts. Even the headmaster can't scare the little girl though.

The birds never taught the little girl fear. You, too, were in some way raised by birds, Jenny. Exactly how is something else you'll need to work out on your own. To help you with that, here's a phrase that will fit on your refrigerator whiteboard: Journey to the nest, enter the cellar.

Jottings from my Moleskine

Intelligence filtered through the heart is pretty neat.
Did I read that somewhere or make it up? Does it matter? Ha! Free-floating wisdom!

I'm at Safeway. Me and this other guy have gotten into two different lines at the same time. That means that, after sizing up the length of the lines, the groceries of the other customers, and the cashiers, we'd come to two different conclusions about which one would be fastest. Now it was on, a contest of his line selection skills versus mine. Our carts were neck and neck until a woman ahead of him started arguing with the cashier—just as I knew she would—about the advertised sale price of her three dozen cans of low-magnesium Friskies. Just then I got called over by a cashier who'd opened up another lane. So, yeah, I got out of the store before the other guy, but I feel cheated of a more clear-cut victory. Am I being petty?

LINER NATE

Dear Nate,

Not at all. Having honed the skill of cashier selection over the course of long personal experience, you feel understandably frustrated about not being able to fully express these skills. In suddenly resolving the story in your favor, the deus ex machina of a new cashier deprived you of the victory that would have felt more genuine for having come through your own powers of discernment.

Oh, and let's all take this opportunity to remind ourselves to beware of the insidious ageism that may creep into the cashier selection process. Feel free to steer clear of coupon-wielding seniors in line ahead of you, just don't resort to negative feelings about their inability to complete a single transaction that doesn't involve calling the assistant manager over for a debate about the fine print in the weekly special.

While we're being ware of that, Nate, your job is to beware of this: the corrosive power of regret in your life. Put the cashier who might have been out of your mind and be grateful for the cashier who is.

Jottings from my Moleskine

I open a Word document. I check the word count. I close the Word document. A little dialogue box asks if I want to save my changes. What changes? Have I altered the object simply by measuring it? Heisenberg haunts Redmond? What other questions can I ask myself about this?

I'm in my neighbor's apartment to feed his dog while he's on vacation. He left insanely detailed instructions, but my question is about the "notes to myself" he has taped to his refrigerator. Would it be unethical for me to copy them down? They're pretty funny and I want to make use of them in my writing.

AUTHOR ARTHUR

Dear Arthur,

Are you telling me there's something funny about "getting in touch with my body wisdom" and "focusing on my gifts for the world"? I guess you should be congratulated since you apparently never need to be reminded to "Simply be" or "Find your 'now' now." Some of us, however, need to reach for a helping hand to get through the day, and the nearest hand is often our own. Perhaps your own method of feeling better is to scoff at others. I'm not going to stand here and tell you that's not a valid approach. Poking at the soft underbelly of your neighbor's guilelessly exposed inner life, however, does seem like a betrayal. On the other hand, the proverb "Never trust a writer" should also be considered in this case.

At my office, a certain individual likes to print articles from the Web that he thinks are ironic/funny/newsworthy and put them up on the office refrigerator for all to enjoy. Problem is, his sources of online content are not compatible with mine. My strategy has been to remove the articles anonymously after enough time has passed that everyone in the office has seen them, but I'd rather not see them at all. What should I do?

FROSTY THE STAKEHOLDER

Dear Frosty,

Something I've contemplated while gazing at the bodhisattva figure in the stairwell of my town house may be of use to you here. While we in the West are blinded by the illusion of permanence, the East teaches that there are no objects, only events. What we think of as a "thing" is in a continual process of arising, abiding, and disintegrating. This is doubly true of a refrigerator, for it's both an event and a conduit for information about other events.

You can also conceive of the refrigerator as an island radio station. It's broadcasting to the little isolated community made up of you and your co-workers, as well as the odd salesperson and copy repair guy who may drift through like foreign sailors. As with any medium of information, whether it's on an island or any other geographical body, the refrigerator must adhere to certain basic guidelines.

I'm not suggesting that anyone try to curtail free speech as practiced on the surface of appliances. On the contrary, my point is that free speech should be *supercharged*—with the power of respect. For we can only truly speak freely when we respect each other. That's just Karma 101. Your co-worker clearly doesn't respect your sensitivity to this truth. Respect can only be achieved by consensus. Consensus is achieved by process. Process is achieved by committee. So form a committee, make a list of Web sites that are acceptable as sources of refrigerator content, compose yourselves into a mob, walk over to his cube, and present your list to your co-worker. That, too, will be an event.

I saw a car with both a "Co-exist" bumper sticker and a Darwin fish eating a Jesus fish. Isn't that a contradiction?

AUNT LOUISE

Dear Louise,

The Darwin fish could possibly be giving the Jesus fish a friendly little hug with its jaws. "Oh, Jesus fish!" the Darwin fish could be saying. "Come here and let me affectionately gnaw on your scaly little head while I explain how your life is based on lies."

How should I greet someone who's wearing earbuds?

SOCIABLE SALLY

Dear Sally,

First, frown and hug yourself tight to represent to the earbud user their own unhealthy electronic cocooning. Second, jump up and stretch out your arms and legs like a joy-crazed starfish greeting the dawn. This will remind the user of the big, w-i-d-e, wonderful world they're missing out on. Then toss your scarf over your shoulder, blow a kiss, and be on your way.

Why does everyone want to sit in a booth?

WAITRESS JUANITA

Dear Juanita,

Eating at a restaurant is special to the extent that it's fancier than eating at your own house. And just as restaurant food is fancier than the food you cook, a booth is fancier than your dining table. It's like a misting of banana oil for your butt.

The preposition a booth takes points to the other reason it's special. You can't sit or lie "in" anything but a booth. There are hammocks, I guess. We had one of those when I was a kid. I only remember lying in it once, back in the summer when we first got it, staring at tree branches against the sky. It's hard to get in those things. They're tippy. You have to sort of trust and get in all at once. I'm pretty sure there's a lesson in there. After that first summer, our hammock was always wet and full of leaves. Then one day it was gone. Not sure about the lesson there.

It's easy to get into a booth though. Its soft yet firm receptivity offers just the right amount of friction as you slide in. Once you're in, you can say you're "ensconced." Which makes it sound like this is something the booth is doing to you. I've always been sort of thrilled by the idea of the booth taking control and ensconcing me. Sometimes it's still warm from its last occupant. I find that sort of unsettling. But the booth is soon filled with a warmth that's all mine.

Maybe in the course of reading those, you started to get a warm feeling yourself when realized that you, too, are among the ranks of the Accidental Seekers. That we all are. How quickly you catch on! I think we're ready to take this theme to the proverbial next level.

The Others Ether

Someone just asked you for directions. You are now in an encounter that seems routine but is packed with spiritual growth potential for all parties. Indeed, it's nothing less than an opportunity to restore people's faith in humanity. And to give yourself a rosy glow of satisfaction. So whatever you do, don't make it simple.

Sure, you could point and tell them where to turn, and that may even be what they think they want. Instead, be as detailed as possible, without limiting yourself to some schematic, closed-minded idea about what's "relevant." Go over the directions twice, the second time illustrating each step with elaborate hand motions. Whip out your Moleskine and draw a map with sketches of major landmarks and arrows pointing out the whimsical details along the route. If you know a foreign language, offer to explain everything again in that language. Walk part of the way with them, to make sure they've really got it. While you're walking, tell them funny stories about the history of the neighborhood. This is your moment to shine! Send them away with the feeling that they just won the lottery of random kindness. Let me phrase that in a slightly more urgent way: If you send them away with anything less than this feeling, are you really doing your best to lead a life of intentionality?

Jottings from my Moleskine

Found myself missing wrong numbers. Everyone on speed dial now. That brief, random connection with another soul—now a thing of the past. Miss especially delivering my joke: "No, he's not here. Try calling his number."

Sorry! I was starting to get a little preachy there. I guess I'm still fired up from the afternoon I spent recently with a German family in matching biker jackets who were trying to find Pike Place Market.

I bring this up because at this point I'm going to rap at you a little about the mysterious medium through which we connect to others: the Others Ether. As we'll see in these letters, optimizing your connections through this ether can make for some pretty magical moments.

I just love going to yard sales. But sometimes I'll stop by a sale and immediately realize there's nothing but a stained old "World's Best Dad" mug, a dusty box of Auto World *magazines, and Volume Two of* Billy Joel's Greatest Hits. *How soon can I leave without being rude?*

SMART SHOPPING SUZY

Dear Suzy,

There are three basic kinds of yard sales. There's the kind held by people who're moving and have lots of stuff priced to move. One step down is the kind held by people who are cleaning out their attic. You might find something good, but it's pretty hit-and-miss. Then there are the sales put on by the bored and the lonely. They don't have anything anyone would want to buy, but they need something to do. More than your money, they just want a little bit of your time. If you so much as glance at that stained old Playskool choo-choo, they'll launch into an account of their son who played with it back in the seventies, and how he lives in Denver now and has kids of his own and doesn't visit very often.

If you want to escape, you can use the cover of someone else's arrival. Or you can pretend that you've got a cell-phone call and back away while smiling apologetically. That old guy in the lawn chair will be fine even if you can't spare a few minutes for a neighborly chat about the weather. Even if most of his friends have died and he's got no plans for the rest of the day. But maybe it's more important for you to get to the post office before it closes. Your call.

Jottings from my Moleskine

How much eye contact is appropriate?
Don't ask! Remember the millipede!

You're old enough, you must remember when we used to sit in peo-
ple's living rooms and watch their slide shows. God, what a bore.
Now we get links to everyone's online photos instead. Who has time
to look at all that stuff?

                                            MOOSEWOOD COOKBOOK

Dear Moosewood Cookbook,

Let's take a little stroll through the backyard of your
question. Oh look, what a coinkydink! There seems to be
a slide show going on inside the house right now! You can
tell from the way the curtains light up with a soft glow of
shifting whites, blues, and tans. Let's step softly so as to not
disturb the people inside. Now we're in the garden, where
we find, folded up in a neat little square and stuffed into the
knot of a pear tree, the answer to your question.

What was your question again? "How can I blow off
friends?"—was that it? Ha, sorry, just giving you a friendly
little poke in the ribs there, Moosewood Cookbook. I know
that wasn't how you phrased it. But did you notice that hushed
sense of calm just now, while we were taking our imaginary
little walk? And how good it felt, especially in contrast to the
frazzled tone you started with? Now, here in the garden, in the
cool of the twilight, let's unfold that paper. It says . . . Well, I
could tell you what it says, but I think you already know.

Seriously, though, if someone sends you one of those
links, all you have to do is comment on just one of the pic-
tures. Something like, "You're making me envious with that
one of you guys in Los Cabos! Good times!" Choose a picture near the end so it appears as though you looked at all
of them.

OK, I know that if I spend any time whatsoever complaining about
Facebook it means I should get a life, but what is it about people who
must narrate the most trivial events of their life? They post status

updates like "About to have a cup of tea!" and then everyone is sup-
posed to click "Like" and comment "Girl, I'm so glad you're taking
some time for yourself!"

                                          TRIVIALLY PURSUED

Dear Pursued,

Hooray for me! It's such a simple sentiment, and yet such an important one for maintaining one's self-esteem. I grant you that some people seem to lead this little cheer for themselves whenever they eat blueberries, go for a bike ride, or listen to the Shins ("Rediscovering their second album"). But is it so wrong to bask in the warm rays of self-validation? And would it really be so hard for you to click "Like"? If you really think so, maybe it's time for you to take off that grumpy adult mask of yours and remember how you felt the first time you made a poo poo in the toilet by yourself.

I recently attended a play, and the performance was mediocre at best.
During the intermission, audience members who were sitting far
enough away from the stage that the performers couldn't plainly see
them quietly gathered up their belongings and did not come back. But
at the end of the play, those of us who remained rose for the inevitable
standing ovation. How bad does a performance have to be these days
before the audience withholds a standing ovation?

                                          UPRIGHT RELUCTANTITE

Dear Upright,

You sound a little frustrated. But here's something you might consider: Performers make themselves incredibly vulnerable when they appear onstage, toiling at their craft for your entertainment. While you sit on your rear end, you big lazybones! Joshing aside, please remember that these performers' sense of self-worth is in your hands. And they are doing their best. Did you stop to think that they are doing their best? Those "mediocre" performers simply can't do any better. How do you think that feels?

But hey, maybe you're right. Maybe when a performance falls short of perfection, we should stay seated. In fact, why stop there? Do a little research on the performers before you go. Then you can shout out taunts tailored to their personal history and ethnic background. "Nice performance, Jewish Guy!" you can shout. "Much like when you prematurely ejaculated into your girlfriend last night!" Sure, that might not make him feel very good, but it would make you feel good. And apparently that's the most important thing here. Or *is* it???

My laid-off friend has been spending her time knitting scarves for everyone she knows. But they're pretty bad scarves. Do we have to wear them?

I FEEL SILLY ABOUT MY NECK

Dear Silly About My Neck,

I've managed to keep my job so far, thank Shiva, but I know a lot of people who haven't. So far these people have managed to keep their spirits up pretty well. Along with a blow-softening severance package, there seems to be a certain giddiness that helps ease the shock of termination, an element of "Haha, imagine *me* getting laid off!" I endorse this giddiness, but worry that it may be harder to maintain the proper spirit of levity as weeks of idleness pile up. Everyone with a laid-off friend should do as much as possible to help that friend stay loose and positive. Because anxiety won't help anything. What this means for you, Silly, is that you do indeed have to wear that lumpy green and orange scarf. Because it's liable to get a lot colder before it warms up.

OK, time to die!

Not really. At least, not yet. But this is something that must be contemplated in the course of any spiritual journey. My mom used to tell me death is part of life, and to reject it is to reject life. I can't improve on that. But a few slightly more *specific* issues have come up for my readers:

> *My friend, who is from a tropical island country, sometimes asks her dead brother to help her win the lottery. "I bring you flowers," she says. "Give me the numbers." Comments?*
>
> *A LOTTO MADNESS*

Dear Lotto,

I really hate to judge someone else's spirituality, but that's pretty materialistic, don't you think? And all too typical of the crass side of Christianity. Whatever happened to the camel and the eye of the needle? But wait, where did you say your friend's from? Is it a foreign country with a vibrant culture? It may not be possible to make a comment here. Vibrancy equals clemency.

> *I'm at the funeral reception of a friend. As a way to feel his presence, we're listening to his iPod on shuffle. So far, so tender. But then this horrendous, squawking free-jazz thing comes on. A glance at the little progress bar tells me it's forty-five minutes long. Annoying, sure, but it was also giving a false impression of my friend as having pretentious taste in music. I knew Josh as well as anyone, and I can tell you that no matter how adventurous his downloading habits, he would have been the first to make fun of himself for playing this bad rehash of Ascension. So I hit forward on the iPod and the next song was "Blackbird" by the Beatles. Sad, beautiful, and everyone likes it.*

In other words, perfect for the occasion. So I should have been a hero,
right? Why did everyone look at me like that?

GRIEVING GREGORY

Dear Gregory,

Small world! I was there, too. I knew Josh because I was
a customer of his when he was waiting tables at that breakfast place on top of Queen Anne. I guess I was on his e-mail
list—maybe from the time he invited me to a show of his
drawings?—because I got the notice his girlfriend sent out
after the accident.

The reaction to what you did at the funeral was indeed
hostile. The collective judgment was that you were violating
the spirit of Josh himself, as represented by his iPod's shuffle
function. What you needed was a clearer communication
strategy. A sheepish smile and the explanation that "he told
me he hated this" would have done the trick. Your decision
to instead celebrate your heroism with a series of fist pumps
and a strutting rooster dance was what turned the crowd
against you.

Have you ever "scattered" someone's ashes? The word gives you
an image of the ashes being spontaneously taken up by the wind to
rejoin nature in a mystical twinkle. The first time I had to deal with
human ashes, I discovered they're heavier than expected, and that
you "scatter" them straight down into an inert pile. Then you stand
around awkwardly, exchange hugs with friends, and walk away.
Now I've got a second set of ashes and want to do a better job. How
should I proceed?

SCATTER BRAINED SCOTTY

Dear Scotty,

Hmm . . . That's a toughie! My first thought is of the sand bluffs of Seattle's Discovery Park. I can't think of a better place to rejoin nature, no matter how imperfectly. And it's often windy enough that you might actually achieve the picturesque effect you describe. Even if you don't see an actual mystical twinkle.

Still, you may be on to something there with your objection to the word "scattering." It raises expectations, doesn't it? And who needs that when someone close to you has just died? That's why you should remember that awkward hugs may be the best anyone can muster. And that's OK. You might also consider not using *all* the ashes in the scattering. It's easier to be ceremonious with a handful than the whole box. Giving yourself a break would also be a good idea about now.

My boyfriend, who's in his late thirties, has recently developed a keen interest in local history. Is this a sign of impending geezerhood?
JOSEPHINE THE SINGER

Dear Josephine,

Often occurring in males, but by no means restricted to them, interest in local history is indeed a sign of aging. The onset of this condition, which can occur anywhere between the ages of thirty-five and fifty-five, is caused by the human mind seeking to adjust to its own mortality. As it senses its limits, the mind naturally seeks out the larger patterns it's part of, and which will continue after it's gone.

You see, Josephine, no one can cope with infinity all at once. It's better to start with the story of the city's first professional fire department and expand into gradually larger time frames. One can eventually develop a vision of personal oblivion as peaceful as the primeval forest that once grew here.

Gardens in my neighborhood are dominated by perennials—subtle, elegant, woodsy plants that bloom, for the most part, once a season. They're great, and they seem so in tune with the understated Northwest ethos. But sometimes when I go to garden stores, I'm tempted by the brighter, flashier annuals that last all season long. Will I seem like a gaudy outsider if I plant them?

BETTY "BUMBLE" BEE

Dear Betty,

I'm on record as being against anyone faking cancer, except perhaps in certain romantic role-playing situations. So please refrain from this, even if it seems like the obvious solution. It will, however, be OK for you to subtly intimate to your perenniaphile neighbors that you're not sure how much time you've got left in this world. Because you don't! No one does. "The light is precious while it lasts," you can say while gazing at the evening sky, or "Ah, sweet thief of time! How consistently dost thou roll on!"

When they learn to approach you and your mysterious condition with a little more respect, then you can let your neighbors in on the joke: They, too, could die anytime! And the whole idea of a perennial that lasts indefinitely is fundamentally flawed! This will help them appreciate petunias, no matter how fleeting, and eventually realize that, in a sense, we're all annuals.

No, but really—what *does* happen when we die?

It's hard to believe from the way I've been yammering on here, but I do know that there's a time to talk and a time to let your silence do the talking. And that's where my tattoo comes in. A lot of people get tattoos as a fashion thing, or to be "edgy" or whatever. There's nothing wrong with that. It's just that I happened to put a little more thought into my own tattoo. It's the Chinese characters for "Peace" framed in an interlaced Celtic pattern. Call me crazy, but I think it's important to be open to wisdom from *all* cultures. Just doing my part to subvert the dominant paradigm, that's all.

I try not to talk about my views too much, but every once in a while I'll casually roll up my sleeve and wait for someone to ask, "Hey what's with that tattoo?" This can be a useful point of departure for elevating the conversation above the usual gossip about reality television programs. "The world becomes what you teach"—I don't know who said that, but I definitely believe it.

Of course, usually no one mentions my tattoo, even if I jut my arm forward suggestively. And that's fine. People aren't always as receptive as you'd like, and you have to roll with that. Bide your time. I should know, I've gotten plenty of practice. If they gave out patches for Time Biding, I'd make Eagle Scout for sure. Joe Bidin', that's what they call me. But I'm in a positive place about it.

It's hard to be positive about death, though, even remembering what my mom said about it. That's why I don't want to finish here without taking the question up directly: What happens when we die? The question of death is the question of life, and I salute you for your bravery in asking. For it is truly a terrifying mystery that spreads above all of humanity like a great eagle silhouetted against the sun. Will I pretend to have the answer? No, I won't. But will I presume to make a suggestion anyway? Yes, I will: Even as it floats with an evil persistence between us and the noonday sun of our everyday bustle, take courage from the noble shape of this hovering silhouette. For just as this shadow threatens to overwhelm your existence, so, too, does the sun looming behind it threaten to overwhelm its inky blackness with a blazing glory. The struggle of darkness against light mirrors our own struggle against darkness. These two forces are also mirrors of each other, so there's one more level of mirror-ness for you to keep in mind. The mere mirror-ality of all reality, I guess you could call it.

Of course the struggle will only continue to produce more shadow and more light. And where does that leave us? With an inextricable mixture of both. Salt and pepper. Yin and yang. Cake and coffee. John and Paul. What is any of them without the other? The trick is to enjoy the light, even mixed as it is with darkness. Like I said, I don't have any answers, but I suppose if you pressed me on the issue, I'd say I'm a bit of a we-live-on-in-hearts-and-minds man myself. At least we know from direct experience that people do live on in our hearts, as surely as we remember our first cookie. I guess what I'm trying to say is, I love you, Mom, wherever you are.

In Conclusion: Some final thoughts

So that's pretty much it.

Now that the book is done, it's back to my day job. I know I'm lucky to even have a job. The job market is looking—*everything* is looking—a bit bleak right now. There's no reason, however, for us to take this bleakness into our spirits.

People here in the Pacific Northwest are known to suffer from SAD, which is when you're sad that it's winter and dark all the time. I like to remind them that the sun isn't as inaccessible as they might think. There's a full spectrum of goodness in even the most overcast skies, and the sun's blessings may be no farther than a brisk afternoon walk away. I'd like to think that lightness of spirit is one of your "take-aways" from this time we've had together.

Maybe, however, it's just the opposite for you. Maybe all my friendly reminders have made you feel, on the contrary, heavy and burdened. And you feel this way knowing *full well* that I have endeavored to deliver my material in as fun a manner as possible. That's totally fine. It wouldn't be very professional of me to take that personally, would it? No, freedom of thought is one right no one can take from you. Please think whatever you want.

But in that case I do have one last suggestion for you: Go take a *rumspringa*. You know, how Amish young people are allowed, for a set period of time, to drink, smoke, and otherwise break the rules of their community? You, too, should take a complete break from the principles we've talked about here. Show that you can "loosen up" with the best of them. Stop recycling. Drink macrobrews and watch professional sports. Drive everywhere. Don't wave when someone lets you change lanes. Kill spiders in your house rather than trapping and freeing them in a silently improvised ceremony of karmic self-blessing. Do all your shopping at Wal-Mart and have them octuple-bag everything. Walk around with a cell phone pressed to your ear at all times, even if no one's on the line, and say things like, "Yeah, that's one sales forecast I'd like to see, let me tell you what, you crazy bastard! You still in for tonight, you miserable cocksucker? Shooters at Hooters, my friend, shooters at Hooters!" Do this at every farmer's market in town. Put down your phone only long enough to tell the Vietnamese farmer that his organic tomatoes are lumpy and not as red as the ones at Safeway. Ask Grease Monkey for all their used oil and pour it into the gutter in front of your house while glaring defiantly at your neighbors. Rent a Hummer and tailgate Vespas. Lean on the horn and call out, "Get a car, Fancy Man!" Name your dog "Fucko" and make him walk around in a suit of chain mail on hot days. Hitch him to a wagon and make him pull you in it. Snap a whip over his head and scream things like "Move yer ass, Fucko!" and "I'ma cut your balls off all over again, Fucko!" At the end of your *rumspringa*, please report back to me as to whether it made you happier or not.

Except I guess you can't on account of we're saying good-bye now. I hope you can make it out for a visit to Seattle sometime. Unless you already live here. In either case, perhaps we may someday exchange tense smiles as we pass on the sidewalk. When you can't find yourself on the x-axis, I'll be the one sending you discreet hand signals about who should use which side of the sidewalk. Follow my hastily improvised pantomime and together we'll have a prance at the whole let's-not-collide thing.

Epilogue

Back to the day job

What office supplies should we reorder?

CO-WORKING CARL

I'm going to back a dark horse on this one, Carl: rubber bands. They sort of fly under the office supplies radar, don't they? They're certainly not as prominent as copy machine paper or whiteboard markers. But when you really need one, there's no substitute for a rubber band. Like when you've got a teetering stack of letters and you want to make it a tidy bundle so badly it makes your brain itch. That's a bad feeling. It's a rubber band–shaped hole in your spirit, is what it is.

I certainly support the decision to start ordering the environmentally friendly ones, the Green-Os, even though they tend to break. Can I tell you something though? I have a whole box of the old ones in my desk. So if you need one sometime, feel free to ask. No, I'm not going to "just give you a handful of them." I said if you need *one* sometime, I'd be more than happy to give you *one* at that time. As long as this doesn't happen more than, say, a couple times a month.

No, I'm not hoarding. That is incorrect. Ten dry-erase markers in your bottom drawer, that's hoarding. Like, ahem, she whom we know whom I mean whom! This box of rubber bands, on the other hand, is no more than a supply I might reasonably expect to need for my own personal use. I know the policy. I'm definitely in fair territory here.

Ooh! You know what we should order? As a gag? Some of those jumbo paper clips. Then at the end of the next meeting of Larry's direct reports, we can say, "Oops, we almost forgot, there's one more thing," then take out a stack of papers labeled "Lawsuit Against Larry" with the jumbo paper clip on it.

What do you mean you're "not feeling it"? What is that expression even supposed to mean? OK, fine. If you don't want to lighten your chi with the therapeutic application of humor, that's the brand of mouthwash you're stuck with, my friend. But, oh! I almost forgot! Do you have like two or three hours this afternoon to help me with that PowerPoint presentation?

Thanks

Kazuko, Kaia, Mom, Dad, Mark Fefer, Brian Miller, Mike Seely, Nina Shapiro, the *Seattle Weekly*, Rod Filbrandt, Jessica Sindler, Kate Lee, Mike Stoesz, Sarah Stoesz, Bess Imber, Katie Doemland, Nicole Ghazal, Cynthia Chapman, Geof Miller, Porter Hall, Tim Sirotnik, Tim Dempsey, Allan Hockett, Stuart Rivchun, Scott Kuhlman, Marcela Valdes, Elizabeth Jameson, Li Ravicz, Grant Fjermedal, Lorraine Johnson, John Stanley and Irving Tripp, Markos and Stef, Loretta and Marc, Helen and Dick, Bonnie and Clyde, Tom Wolfe, B. R. Myers, Knute Berger, Murray Morgan, *New Spirit Journal*, *Conscious Choice Magazine*, Suzzallo Library, Greenwood Library, the continuously sighing guy in the Greenwood Library, Microsoft, Candy Floss, Mr. Gyros, Mae's Tofu Breakfast, Herkimer Coffee, Spudka Vodka, Marguie, Peter, the Rude Pop Deities, the Head Monkeys, the Witchita Lineman, the Cascades over the Lake, and the Olympics over the Sound.

About the author

The Uptight Seattleite majored in Japanese Studies and has a masturbator's degree in Comparative Religion. He is a thinker, a writer, a seeker, and a columnist for the *Seattle Weekly*. His yoga practice is his laughter practice is his personal revolution. He believes in discovering beauty and weaving it into transformation. He believes in the power of active listening. Shh! Hear that? It's the sound of your own listening! He has been single for many years.

About the illustrator

Rod Filbrandt lives in Vancouver and is the author of *Dry Shave*, a collection of his noir- and booze-soaked comics.